Two Rivers from a Common Spring

Two Rivers from a Common Spring

The Books Council of Wales at 60

Edited by Gwen Davies

Linocuts by Molly Brown

CYNGOR LLYFRAU CYMRU
BOOKS COUNCIL of WALES

CYNGOR LLYFRAU CYMRU
Castell Brychan
Aberystwyth
SY23 2JB
https://llyfrau.cymru

First published 2021
© Copyright (text): the contributors, translators, the Books Council of Wales
© Copyright (illustrations): Molly Brown

ISBN (print) 978-1-914981-01-2
ISBN (ebook) 978-1-914981-04-3
A sister volume to this one, *O Hedyn i Ddalen: Dathlu'r Cyngor Llyfrau yn 60*, is available, ISBN 978-1-914981-00-5 (print), ISBN 978-1-914981-03-6 (ebook)
Design and typesetting: Olwen Fowler
Cover image: 'Two Rivers' by Molly Brown
Images for endpapers: 'Hart's Tongue Fern' by Molly Brown
Printed and bound in Wales by Gwasg Gomer, Llandysul, Ceredigion, Wales

Published with the generous financial support of the Creunant family

A CIP catalogue for this book is available from the British Library

In memory of Alun Creunant

Contents

Wales (plural)

*Charting our book trade
through a pandemic and towards
a pluralistic Wales*

Wales (plural)

Helgard Krause on charting our book trade
through a pandemic and towards
a pluralistic Wales

It is both an honour and a pleasure to introduce this volume charting and celebrating the first sixty years of this organisation, which I have been leading for the last four years. To my own family at the time, my appointment as Chief Executive may have seemed intriguing. That I, as a German woman, who only moved to Wales in my thirties, would be heading such an important Welsh national institution! But those closer to the Books Council may well, perhaps, have seen how such a move in fact exemplifed the ambitious and outward-looking ethos which has propelled the organisation since its inception, and it speaks volumes that during the sixty years of its existence I was proceeded by only three directors (Alun Creunant Davies, Gwerfyl Pierce Jones and Elwyn Jones) who all tackled very different but crucial challenges during their tenures. From the moment of its inception, the Council had to be alive to the needs of this ever expanding, dynamically changing, bilingual publishing sector in Wales, and, in particular, to the challenges that face English-language publishers operating in the most competitive of global markets.

This book is indeed one that charts a history. But there is no element here, in its due celebration of the past, of resting on laurels. Rather, *Two Rivers from a Common Spring* inspires us to hold on to our strategic purpose. But also to nurture critical self-reflection, openness and cooperation, qualities which I hope my leadership embodies.

Almost immediately upon taking up this role in 2017, I appeared in front of the Culture, Welsh Language and Communications Committee of the Assembly, to respond to the recommendations of Professor Medwin Hughes's *Independent Review of Support for Publishing and Literature in Wales*. Four years on, the changes it instigated are bearing fruit but, more importantly perhaps, it also led to strengthened relationships with other organisations who support the wider literature sector in Wales.

The year 2020 was one of the most challenging periods for our organisation, the sector we serve, colleagues, friends, families and for Wales as a whole. It is hard to believe that more than a year has passed since the uncertainties of the early days of lockdown which required us to make and change plans, hourly, at times. There are so many moments, seemingly insignificant, that are etched in my memory. It may sound surprising, but by now I consider many of the disruptions and changes we faced then as being ultimately positive, in that they instigated a substantial rethinking of our work and priorities, as well as bringing about real innovation.

The pleasure and transformative power of reading and its tangible benefits for our mental health was brought into sharp relief as other leisure pursuits remained severely curtailed. Many of us were reminded of or discovered the respite a printed book can bring after long hours learning, teaching or working in front of a screen. Armchair travelling took on a whole new meaning. Many of us visited anew old friends which had lingered neglected on our bookshelves.

Our new digital platform, Ffolio, was conceived and realised in less than six months, answering the urgent calls from schools and libraries for more such content (including ebooks), especially for children in Welsh-medium education who may not have had the benefit of a Welsh-speaking parent at home. In this context, the importance of audio books for all learners of Welsh – irrespective of age – was also highlighted during the year. Due to market failure, this will require an assertive policy and funding intervention; we are in discussion with Welsh Government to consider the next steps.

Our organisation was founded to support the publishing industry in Wales, and in so doing, has had to adapt, over and again. But rarely, if ever, did it have to embrace change at such a rapid pace as during the last year, and to do so without the careful planning that usually proceeds business or organisational change. The early days of the pandemic were consumed with the logistical challenges of supporting half of our colleagues as they adjusted to remote working, while also keeping our distribution services running. Without those services, it would have been nigh on impossible to buy Welsh-language books during lockdown.

Our strategic long-term cooperation with Welsh Government meant that we were able to contribute to emergency funding conditions, re-opening guidance and additional financial support. We secured substantial investment from Welsh Government's Education Department, to provide health and wellbeing books for schools, while also working closely with several local authorities to support vulnerable families and children with book parcels, as well as coordinate a national scheme to provide additional books for libraries. The positive impact of such schemes is manifold, as they benefit not only readers and learners, but also the entire supply chain which is part of the foundational economy in Wales, and includes authors, publishers and booksellers.

In a long-established organisation such as ours, there is always a delicate balance to strike between respecting and building on past achievements, while also being courageous enough to make changes where necessary. We must engage in a meaningful way to remove any barriers within our systems that exclude those from underrepresented and diverse communities from accessing opportunities that will develop their talent and support their ambitions.

Early summer 2020 confronted us with the truly shocking footage of the murder of George Floyd and the public outcry that reverberated around the world. #BlackLivesMatter demanded of us all that we face up to questions many should have asked sooner. For me, the movement led to real soul searching and self-examination, and it triggered some challenging discussions within our organisation, the wider sector and throughout Wales. The shocking racist graffiti, which defaced our head office in Aberystwyth in March 2021, served as a further grim reminder of how much there is still to do. To add to these complex issues, that white supremacist graffiti (of an unfortunate, ill-informed Welsh hue) also highlighted what could be interpreted as a colonial blind spot within our culture and institutions, around language and equalities. This particular dialogue is fraught with difficulties, but it makes it all the more urgent. We look forward to the fruits of projects such as Hunan-Iaith (outlined in Hanan Issa's thoughtful essay and which, among other things has produced a glossary of Welsh-translated terms relating to People of Colour). Such initiatives are to be welcomed, in that they will help us, as an institution, to facilitate and participate in this much-needed national conversation. Above all, we must work against competing hierarchies of oppression, both old and new. Instead, we must move to inhabit a place where honest and inclusive celebration can happen, clear of conscience. Such a place, in its books and in its practices, will reflect a genuinely diverse Wales, to which people from all walks of life – from all sorts of background, and with all types of experience – can feel that they belong.

Transformational change takes time, especially in an industry such as ours, built as it is upon the inspiration and creativity of writers and illustrators, as well as the longer-term development of new voices and the deep and detailed work of editors. I am determined that when we look back on our seventieth year, we will have witnessed substantial and sustained change in both the industry we support and within our own organisation. Only when we can confidently say that not a single part of our community here in Wales is underrepresented – be they poets, authors, editors, designers, illustrators or marketeers – will we be able to celebrate our achievements, hand on heart.

Addressing our own fundament, we have taken steps to strengthen our corporate and legal structures as well as governance arrangements, which in March 2021, led to the appointment of seven new trustees who bring a wealth of experience and skills that will enable us to navigate the challenges of the coming years.

I very much appreciate the steadfast support of former members of our executive committee and council, without which we could not have delivered our services as effectively. I especially thank our chief officers who supported us in making the necessary changes. I am deeply grateful for the tireless voluntary work of our panel members, awards judges and the Friends of the Books Council.

I am indebted to all my colleagues, whose unwavering devotion to our work has helped us succeed during an exceptionally difficult year.

I would like to extend my special thanks to all the contributors, but, in particular, to M. Wynn Thomas, without whom it would not exist. This volume not only demonstrates the lasting impact of the Council's work over the last six decades but also underlines the important future role we hold in ensuring that readers of all ages see themselves, their lives and their country reflected through the content we support. I would also like acknowledge the invaluable work done by the editor, Gwen Davies, in bringing this project to such an impressive conclusion, and also to thank Molly Brown for the exquisite linocuts, as well as Olwen Fowler, for working her magic to make this volume a beautiful object in its own right.

And the last words of thanks rightly belong to the publishers, authors and illustrators who surprise and delight us every day. And, equally, to the booksellers, who ensure that our communities here can buy books from Wales, in both languages, that resonate, reflect (and, yes, sometimes help us escape from) their own lives. It is the sum of this collective endeavour and dedication which makes me look forward to this next chapter in our history.

Helgard Krause was appointed Chief Executive
of the Books Council of Wales in 2017.

The Historical
Background

The Historical
Background

Rhidian Griffiths

Make for yourselves friends of books,
so that when you grow old you will have
some to welcome you when many forsake you.

Emrys ap Iwan

The year 1546 has some claim to be considered a turning point in Welsh history, because it was in that year that *Yny lhyvyr hwnn* [In this book], a collection of religious and other fragments, appeared. It was put together by Sir John Pryse (1502/3–55), a gentleman from Breconshire who enjoyed a successful career in the service of the Crown, and who took a lively interest in the history and language of the Welsh people.

Sir John assembled a library of books and manuscripts, to which he added when he took a leading role in the dissolution of the monasteries in the 1530s. Pryse was a humanist. He embraced the ideals of the Renaissance which had, early on, identified the potential of the printing press devised in Germany in the fifteenth century by Johann Gutenberg, and was anxious that his fellow countrymen should profit from this development. On the face of it, *Yny lhyvyr hwnn* is an unassuming publication, and it would hardly be noticed in any considered survey of the important publications of sixteenth-century Europe.

Yet its significance is considerable, as *Yny lhyvyr hwnn* was the first book to be printed in the Welsh language. Although Welsh was not as such the language of formal learning in the period of the Renaissance and Reformation, the act of linking it to the new art of printing drew it into the modern world, ensuring its place as a language of new technology on a par with classical and other modern languages. Printing was the means of spreading learning and those new religious ideas which were a dominant feature of the sixteenth century. This was the beginning of a long and fruitful relationship between Welsh and the printing press, a momentously important step which helped to ensure the survival of the language, by preventing it from sinking to the level of a patois, or even to complete extinction.

The books of this period were not those of the open market, produced in large quantities to meet the needs of a reading public. They were laboriously printed on hand presses and in limited numbers. The history of the period since 1546 traces the development of the Welsh people's relationship with books, which can be said, by and large, to be an affectionate one. By the nineteenth and twentieth centuries, books would proliferate and be purchased by a greater proportion of the populace than ever before. And yet it was always a battle to produce books in Welsh that could satisfy commercial needs, and only in the last part of the twentieth century was there solid growth in the book trade, following the development of a formal pattern of subsidy.

Yny lhyvyr hwnn is a work of piety, which brings together items of religious import, but it also reveals a humanist desire to use the printing press to disseminate elements of the Welsh literary heritage. Wales's early printed books reflected these two strands, and to some extent set a pattern for Welsh printing for a period of four and a half centuries. *Yny lhyvyr hwnn* belongs more to a reformed Catholic than to a Protestant tradition, and the first Protestant works to be printed were those of William Salesbury. More of the fruits of Renaissance learning were seen in Salesbury's work, especially in his dictionary, *A Dictionary in Englyshe and Welshe* (1547) and his collection of proverbs, *Oll synnwyr pen Kembero ygyd*, published in the same year. His translations of the Book of Common Prayer and the New Testament appeared in 1567; and by the end of the sixteenth century, humanism had produced other standard texts, including the Grammar of Gruffydd Robert, which appeared in Milan in 1567, and the Grammar of Siôn Dafydd Rhys, published in 1592. These may all be counted milestones in the history of the book in Wales.

Yet in this early period it was not the work of William Salesbury, but that of William Morgan, which had the greatest impact on the Welsh people. His classic translation of the Welsh Bible appeared in 1588, and set a standard for written Welsh which still holds good. Morgan's Bible, printed, like other early Welsh books, in London, was not a book for individual readers but an authorised translation to be read in churches of the dioceses of Wales and Hereford, by royal decree of Elizabeth I in 1563; a thousand copies were printed to meet institutional needs. The importance of William Morgan's Bible lay not only in bringing Scripture to the ears of the people in churches and maintaining a standard of literary Welsh, but also in placing Welsh on the same level as other European languages into which Scripture was translated in the sixteenth century.

William Morgan's Bible (in the revised form given to it by Bishop Richard Parry and Dr. John Davies of Mallwyd in 1620), had more influence than any other publication on the development of written Welsh up to the end of the twentieth century. It gave the literary language idioms and expressions which became part of the vocabulary of Welsh authors through the ages. Had not the Protestant Reformation and pride in Welsh literary tradition met in William Morgan's translation, it is likely that the Welsh language and awareness of Welsh identity would have dwindled to nothing.

We should not, however, omit to mention the romance of the first book to be printed on Welsh soil, according to tradition, in a cave. The right to print was regulated by the Crown, and printing could not be undertaken without an official licence. This meant that during the sixteenth century, books were printed legally only in three places: London, Oxford and Cambridge. But because Welsh Counter-reformers did not wish to see all the advantages of the press enjoyed exclusively by Protestants, they attempted to strike back by providing a Catholic text in their native language. *Y Drych Cristianogawl* (1586–87) was printed illegally in Rhiwledyn, near Llandudno, and circulated with a false imprint which claimed that it had been produced in Rouen. In the same way, the works of Gruffydd Robert, printed in Milan, were an attempt to attract the Welsh back to the faith of their fathers. It was partly through books that the tussle for the souls of the Welsh took place in the time of the Reformation and Counter-reformation.

Though the number of readers in this period was small, this was the germ of the idea of Wales as a literate nation. The Welsh language had taken root as the language of print.

Books of this period tended to belong to one stratum of society (humanists and learned ecclesiastics), and it was only by degrees, with the gradual increase in literacy, that the idea of books being the property of the people took root. So little growth was there between 1600 and 1700, that Welsh might well have disappeared completely as the language of print. Only late in the century did the beginnings of a genuine book trade emerge. Yet a new edition of the Book of Common Prayer did appear, in 1621, accompanied by the first printing of the metrical psalms of Edmwnd Prys. This classic versification by the Archdeacon of Merioneth of all 150 psalms represented the first free-metre poetry in Welsh to be put into print, and it also laid the foundations of congregational singing in Wales. Publications such as these had widespread impact through the church, where worshippers would hear the words of the Prayer Book and the Bible and would sing Prys's psalms. Prys's motive was a democratic one, since he is on record as wishing to seek, through his verse, to reach the people, who found it easier to learn a verse of a carol than a cywydd.

Books of the period also reflect the importance of patronage by individuals to support printing costs. A prime example is the publication of a popular edition of the Bible. In 1630, through the sponsorship of two prominent London Welshmen, Sir Thomas Myddelton and Rowland Heilyn, the 'Beibl bach' (little Bible) appeared in a small pocket edition which sold for a crown (five shillings), and which prompted Rhys Prichard ('Vicar Prichard', 1579?–1644) to write:

> The 'little Bible' is now readily To be had in your mother tongue
> for a crown; Sell your shirt rather than be without it, It is better
> than your inheritance to keep you.

This step would enable many more to possess books, but few would sell a shirt for its sake. The verses of Vicar Prichard himself were circulated orally during his lifetime, and it was only in 1658 that they reached print. The 'little Bible' may have opened a way to take the Word to more people, but they were still the literate gentry rather than the common people (only around fifteen to twenty per cent of the population of Wales in 1640 could read).

The second half of the century witnessed the publication of more religious texts – translations of Puritan devotional works, for instance, all printed in London – but towards the end of the century there appeared signs of the fundamental changes that would open up the world of printing and publishing. Following the Restoration in 1660, the Crown monopoly on printing was gradually relaxed. Before 1700, Welsh books began to be printed in Oxford, Cambridge and Dublin as well as Shrewsbury and Chester, though presses in those centres, as in London, could suffer from the absence of printers who understood Welsh and could set it correctly.

In this period too, there was a slow move to commercial printing, less dependent on patronage. But the distribution network for books in Wales was primitive, and it is doubtful whether many of the titles published (around 150 between 1600 and 1700) made much of an impression. Welsh books were printed in the Marches, for instance, by Thomas Jones of Shrewsbury, who published a dictionary, *Y Gymraeg yn ei Disgleirdeb* (Welsh in its lustre) in 1688, and who enjoyed particular success with his almanacks, which offered to a wider audience information that suited their needs.

The seventeenth century also witnessed the beginning of the use of the printing press for polemical and political reasons, chiefly during the Civil War. Many a political tract was printed in defence of parliamentary or royalist standpoints, though in English rather than Welsh. So began the development of the use of the press in a more varied way.

The dawn of the eighteenth century saw a development which had popular consequences for the Welsh book. It was in 1718 that the first work legally printed on Welsh soil appeared, namely *Cân o Senn i'w hên Feistr Tobacco* (A song of rebuke to his old master tobacco), printed on the press of Isaac Carter at Trefhedyn near Newcastle Emlyn. The significance of this event is far greater than the size of this printed two-page ballad might suggest. For one thing, it was the first fruit of the development and dissemination of the craft of printing in Wales. The fact that the press was established in a small rural township rather than in a more populous urban area is symbolic of what would be the nature of much

Welsh printing after 1718; because although towns such as Carmarthen, Swansea and Llanidloes developed into printing centres, much printing continued in villages, giving the Welsh press a unique character.

That this press's first product was a ballad is important, since ballads and poems – many of them by local poets, and only a few pages long – would come to form a large part of the output of the Welsh press in the eighteenth and nineteenth centuries. Nevertheless, it was from such modest beginnings that there grew a busy industry which would encompass not only ballads and poems but also newspapers and books of substance. If 1546 is a milestone year in the history of Wales and the Welsh language, 1718 deserves to be equally recognised.

It is estimated that over 2,500 Welsh books appeared between 1660 and 1799, some two-thirds of them after 1750, as momentum grew. In the early years of the eighteenth century, printers would issue limited runs of some 200 copies, but by the mid-century there were occasional print runs of 8,000. This period saw not only the foundation of new presses but also the development of their craft and professionalism.

In addition, as the industry became more professional, a change came over the pattern of patronage which had sustained publishing in earlier generations. By the eighteenth century, the old landowning families were being subsumed by larger estates, and their owners were setting their sights on London. Although some families continued to interest themselves in things Welsh and would contribute to publication costs, not so much was to be expected from the anglicised Welshmen of the eighteenth century. But the interest of many literary-minded London-based gentry continued, and societies like the Cymmrodorion and Gwyneddigion would make an important contribution to literary activity and to publishing. Within Wales itself, the book world became by degrees more 'popular', as native presses grew in response to the numbers and tastes of literate individuals who were buying Welsh-language books. More responsibility was falling on the people of the 'middle class' to disseminate information, and their efforts would count for just as much as gentry patronage.

This eighteenth-century popular revolution was facilitated by the activity of educational charities, that had begun at the end of the previous century.

The establishment of the Welsh Trust in 1674 was a means of promoting literacy through the founding of schools to teach children to read, and arrangements were made to reprint religious and devotional works. This was an attempt to combine the needs of the Welsh people and the ambition of scholars and patrons to get Welsh texts into print. Greater success attended the efforts of the Society for the Propagation of Christian Knowledge (SPCK), established in 1698.

Both bodies subsidised editions of the Welsh Bible and devotional works in Welsh. Although the language of instruction in their schools was English, their activity laid the foundations of the development of literacy in Wales and paved the way for more successful educational schemes. Around 180 schools were established by the SPCK, and it seems very likely, as Melville Richards suggests, 'that there was a significant rise in the number of Welsh people who could read' as a result of the efforts of both organisations. These movements did bring books closer to the people: when the 1718 edition of the Bible appeared, promoted by Moses Williams, who assiduously collected subscriptions for it, 1,000 copies (of the 10,000 printed) were distributed gratis. Having the Bible in their hands was an incentive to ordinary people to learn to read.

What made a significant difference, however, was the success of the circulating schools movement led by Griffith Jones (1684–1761) of Llanddowror, one of the chief educational pioneers in Welsh history, who established over 3,000 schools throughout Wales. Unlike the schools of the Welsh trust and the SPCK, the circulating schools used Welsh – their pupils' mother tongue – as the medium of instruction, which partly accounted for their success. The schools' aims were primarily religious, to instruct children and adults to read the catechism and the Bible, but through Griffith Jones's inspiration and the example given by gifted teachers, much more was achieved. They provided a fillip for churches and the infant Methodist movement, but also a boost to the book trade, as the number of people who could read increased in more than one social class.

The circulating schools came to an end around 1780, but another movement – whose legacy would be even more far-reaching – would inherit their work. Around 1785, the Sunday school movement began to take off, under the leadership of Thomas Charles. Their success in nurturing reading skills – particularly in

Welsh – was such that even the commissioners of the Education Reports of 1847 (the 'Blue Books') were ready to acknowledge the beneficent influence of Sunday schools on the nation. By 1818, 315 Sunday schools had been established in Wales, with a total of 25,000 pupils. These would not all be readers, still less purchasers, of Welsh books; but circulating schools and Sunday schools had between them helped to ensure the existence of a varied readership.

Most of the output of the Welsh press in the eighteenth century was religious and literary, but more books than in the previous century were original Welsh works rather than translations. Among them were volumes of the poetry, hymns and prose works of Morgan Rhys, Dafydd Jones of Caeo and William Williams of Pantycelyn; collections of poetry such as *Blodeu-gerdd Cymry* by Dafydd Jones of Trefriw, and the dictionaries compiled by John Walters and Thomas Richards. Although it is difficult to gauge the popularity of these works in statistical terms, they certainly reached an audience in all parts of Wales.

In this same century came the earliest examples of popular publishing on a substantial scale. The first printing of Peter Williams's Bible appeared, in fifteen parts, at one shilling each, between 1767 and 1770, and achieved sales of 8,600 copies. The practice of publishing larger works in parts was better suited to the needs and character of the Welsh market with its poorer purchasers and the limited resources of its publishers. In spite of the considerable development of the book trade in this period, publishing Welsh books could be a very uncertain business. If Wales possessed a literate audience, it did not of necessity consist of people who were desperate for the opportunity to buy books in their mother tongue. Lewis Morris gave this timely warning to Dafydd Jones of Trefriw when the latter was preparing his *Blodeu-gerdd Cymry*, which appeared in 1759. His words have an almost contemporary ring:

> For the numbers of books you should print, leave that until last, insist
> on seeing first how many subscribers you get. You were dreaming
> when you talked about getting a thousand or fifteen hundred; if you
> get five hundred you will do wonderfully well; especially as pennies
> are so scarce in Wales these days. I know a number of excellent
> authors who could not get more than a hundred or two at most.

This uncertainty influenced the nature of the Welsh book trade, with its extensive dependence on subscription as a means of paying the costs of a publication. Whereas publication in the sixteenth and seventeenth centuries depended on the patronage of gentry and wealthy merchants, the eighteenth century was the age of the subscriber (though the occasional patron still contributed generously). Subscriptions would guarantee the appearance of the first part of a work and then individuals might continue to support it by subscribing to the succeeding parts. The printer would be paid for the first part and would therefore be more confident to undertake the rest of the work. Author and printer would often do their share of collecting subscriptions, although the bulk of the work usually fell to the author. As a rule, lists of subscribers' names appear in the printed volumes, and those lists are a guide to the variety of literate Wales in the period. Reading, or the possession of books, was not simply a gentry pastime: subscription lists of the period reflect a variety of occupations – farmers, carpenters, blacksmiths, drovers and many others.

By the end of the eighteenth century, around fifty presses had been established across Wales. Although many of these were small, and employed very few people, Wales's printers were quite adventurous, and as the century wore on, the standard of their work improved. There were also some interesting experiments, such as the establishment of a press at the religious community at Trefeca in Breconshire. But the industry was still on a limited scale, and the book market depended much on the co-operation and commitment of volunteers to distribute books. William Williams of Pantycelyn took advantage of the network of Methodist societies to market his own books, while wholesale trading was almost entirely in the hands of individuals rather than shops.

It was in this period that people from outside Wales began to be interested in the country, especially its landscape, and by the end of the eighteenth century, English-language travel books singing the praises of the beauty of wild Wales would be coming off the presses. But these were aimed at a wealthy market, not the Welsh people in general, and a quite natural division emerged between Welsh-language and English-language output. It was also during the eighteenth century that presses at Trefriw and elsewhere began to turn out ballads, and produce material that would be a means of promoting and developing popular poetry in Welsh. Such developments were an important contribution to supporting the Welsh language as a book language at every level – the exalted and the popular – and set a pattern for the future.

From around 1820 onwards, presses in Wales began to invest in new machinery and develop into commercial concerns: this was the beginning of the so-called 'golden age' of Welsh printing and publishing. The nineteenth century was a great age of invention and technology, the century of the Great Exhibition of 1851, and the one in which steam presses were developed, enabling printers to produce books more quickly and in greater numbers than ever before. It was a century of movement, especially in relation to the population of Wales, which grew from a little over half a million to over two million between 1801 and 1901, with the growth of industry and the effects of the Industrial Revolution. The growth was most marked in south-east Wales. As a result, many more people were living in towns, and those towns came to house presses. By 1891, 1,541 of those 2,053 people employed by presses in Wales worked in Glamorgan and Monmouthshire. Printing and publishing tended to become urban industries, because it was in towns that the market was biggest and communication easiest, and labour and skills more readily available, while the growth of the middle class and the professions was accompanied by a growth in the number of readers.

Organised religion, especially among the Nonconformists, was one of the hallmarks of the age. By the second half of the nineteenth century, it could be counted a national institution – in 1891, Wales had 4,025 ministers of religion – and much of its life depended entirely on the common people who formed its membership. It is no surprise therefore that the century saw religious publishing on a considerable scale. But there were also lawyers and bankers, as well as manual workers, who enjoyed reading and who possessed books. Among the owners of early Welsh Bibles listed by John Ballinger in his *The Bible in Wales* (1906) we find David Davies, a grocer from Dolgellau, and Thomas Jones, a saddler from Llandeilo.

The nineteenth century was also the most flourishing period of newspapers and periodicals in Wales. English was the medium of the first Welsh newspaper,

The Cambrian, founded in Swansea in 1804, but it was followed in the same town by *Seren Gomer*, first published in 1814, which established the principle of a newspaper in Welsh. Having news in Welsh was a means of developing the interest of the common people in reading, and the nineteenth century would prove to be the golden age of the Welsh-language newspaper. The most important title, and the first to be widely successful, was the politically aware newspaper, *Yr Amserau*, established by Gwilym Hiraethog in Liverpool in 1843. Even more successful was *Y Faner*, founded by Thomas Gee, which was to take over *Yr Amserau*; during the years from 1880 to 1914, the weekly circulation of *Baner ac Amserau Cymru* was 13,000. In addition to these Wales-wide newspapers, a large number of local titles appeared, appealing to a wide spectrum of literate society.

There were also flourishing periodicals, especially religious titles, beginning with *Trysorfa Ysprydol*, established in 1799, which found its place within what became a flourishing market that continued well into the nineteenth century. A particular emphasis within these publications was religious and political controversy, strengthening the habit of thoughtful reading among the Welsh-speaking populace. It has even been suggested that religious controversy was the staple diet of the Welsh people in this period, and that more general reading matter did not command the same attention. But the establishment of *Y Traethodydd* in 1845, under the editorship of Lewis Edwards, marked an attempt to broaden the nation's horizons by emulating English-language literary periodicals like the *Edinburgh Review*: by the end of its first decade, *Y Traethodydd* had attained a circulation of between 1,400 and 1,500 per issue.

By the second half of the nineteenth century, a wider variety of reading was available on different subjects, including lighter publications such as *Y Punch Cymraeg* (1858–64). But it was not until 1891, with the foundation of O.M. Edwards's *Cymru*, with its emphasis on the history, culture and folklore of the Welsh, and its echoes of the nationalism of the Young Wales movement, that a genuinely popular success was achieved in this field. *Cymru* was to spawn other periodicals, especially *Cymru'r Plant*, begun in 1892 and beloved of generations of school pupils who were members of Urdd Gobaith Cymru in the twentieth century. Such periodicals made the most imaginative attempts to provide a wider range of entertaining reading.

To some extent, literate society in the first half of the nineteenth century was divided. The printing house of Thomas Gee of Denbigh, for instance, produced many good quality English-language books, and Welsh-language books on poorer paper, to be sold more cheaply. In the same way, Maria Jane Williams's pioneering collection of Welsh folk-songs, *Ancient National Airs of Gwent and Morganwg*, published by the press of William Rees of Llandovery in 1844, may be viewed as a publication for the gentry. Although it presented Welsh folk-songs with Welsh words, the introduction and notes were in English, and its subscribers were in general wealthy people.

But from the 1860s onward, in particular after the abolition of paper taxes and the development of the steam press, Welsh-language publishing became more substantial, more ambitious, and more popular. In accordance with the fashion of the time, numerous volumes of sermons were published, some of which achieved commercial success. In 1869, Thomas Gee published a collection of the sermons of John Jones of Talysarn, of which at least 10,000 copies were printed.

Gee also attempted to respond to the call for general knowledge by establishing *Y Gwyddoniadur Cymreig*, a Welsh encyclopaedia published in parts between 1854 and 1879, with a second revised edition between 1889 and 1896, a huge venture which showed, according to the eminent scholar Sir Edward Anwyl, the life and vigour of Welsh compared with all other Celtic languages.

Almanacks and handbooks would also sell well, as would some editions of popular poetry such as the works of Mynyddog, published by Hughes and Son of Wrexham. The same publishers enjoyed commercial success following their purchase of the rights to the novels of Daniel Owen in the 1880s and 1890s. It is estimated that up to 10,000 Welsh books were published during the nineteenth century, not counting the many ballads and single sheets of music that appeared, while some popular works were mass-produced – in particular, almanacks, Sunday school commentaries, and popular poetry. Where publishing was linked to contemporary popular culture, substantial sales were assured. Popular anthems and cymanfa ganu programmes could be produced in their thousands, because they were certain to be bought by those who attended those events.

Even so, the publishing industry was rather more fragile than might at first appear. In 1875, Charles Hughes, the proprietor of Hughes and Son, estimated that around £100,000 was spent on Welsh publications of all kinds every year: but though this may appear to be a substantial sum, it was not large in the context of the book trade in other countries, nor, in Hughes's own opinion, in a specifically Welsh context. Although certain periodicals reached the heights in terms of circulation – *Trysorfa y Plant* under the editorship of Thomas Levi could sell 44,000 copies – others did not succeed to the same extent. In the late nineteenth and early twentieth centuries, when Wales's enthusiasm for music was at its peak, music periodicals did not sell well – *Cerddor y Cymry* (1883–94), published in Llanelli under the editorship of W. T. Rees, 'Alaw Ddu' sold at best 900 copies – and *Y Cerddor* would not have lasted as long as it did (in three series from 1889 to 1939), without substantial subsidies from its publisher, Hughes and Son. Welsh people complained that books were expensive (although their prices tended to be lower than those of similar books in English), while others argued that the purchasers were to blame for their unwillingness to pay a realistic price. Such a complaint could apply in any generation, but in the context of the million Welsh speakers recorded in the Census of 1911, better things might be expected. The resources of Welsh publishers were limited, yet there was over-concentration on a too restricted range of subjects, especially religious books (including sermons) and books of unexceptional poetry; people were driven to seek the variety to be found in English books.

Another weakness in this period was the mechanism for distribution. Bookshops were scarce, and publishers depended much on private distributors who were renowned for not paying the publisher's bill, and who sometimes disappeared, leaving their debts unpaid. And because much of the selling was on a limited scale, concern was expressed, as early as 1890, that there was no centre for Welsh books and books about Wales, and that booksellers in Wales found it difficult and tiresome to deal with each publisher separately. In 1913, O.M. Edwards was to propose that a warehouse for wholesale sales to booksellers in Wales and England should be created, to be sited (ironically enough) in London.

Just before the First World War, Hughes and Son reported that the sale of Welsh books had been declining for some years, and no doubt the publishers themselves were guilty of failing to innovate in terms of variety of subject. Though Hughes and Son enjoyed success with the novels of Daniel Owen, and Isaac Foulkes of Liverpool risked publishing series of Welsh classics, publishers in general found it difficult to adjust to the change in public taste at the end of the nineteenth century. In 1912, the journalist E. Morgan Humphreys detected 'a lack of enterprise' among Wales's publishers. And in spite of his success with the periodical *Cymru*, the wizard O.M. Edwards had less luck with his 'Cyfres y Fil', which sought to establish a pattern of Welsh classics at a reasonable price.

No Welsh publishing house (not even the largest of them, Gee of Denbigh and Hughes and Son of Wrexham), could survive on publishing alone, even during their most successful times. All of them relied on additional activities, such as jobbing printing, a shop, or the printing of newspapers, to make ends meet. Hughes and Son also relied on the co-operation of Ballantyne of Edinburgh to print works. It was in England and Scotland that many nineteenth-century Welsh books were produced, such as the illustrated Bibles so popular in Welsh homes, and substantial works such as Kilsby Jones's 1867 edition of the works of William Williams of Pantycelyn, which was energetically sold by the agents of the publisher William Mackenzie.

Another significant development in the world of the book in nineteenth-century Wales was the emergence of public libraries. There were some reading societies in the eighteenth century, serving a limited social circle – one such in Carmarthen by 1752, and another in Merthyr by 1804. In 1831, the Society for the Improvement of the Working Men of Glamorgan was founded, a circulating library with its headquarters in Cowbridge and branches in some south Wales towns; every six months it would lend 25 books to each branch, including material in Welsh, particularly in the field of agriculture. Yet it appears that this was a short-lived venture. In 1850, an act of parliament enabled local authorities to raise a levy on rates to pay for a public library. Wales was in general slow to respond to this opportunity, and it was only in the twentieth century that public libraries would have a significant educational impact on the populace at large.

Cardiff was the first authority to adopt the act, in 1862. It was followed by Newport, Swansea and Wrexham, each one a centre of population, and by two smaller towns where the first constituent colleges of the University of Wales were established, namely Aberystwyth and Bangor. Some of these library collections developed into important research collections, particularly the Cardiff collection, which included a large number of Welsh-language books.

A number of Workmen's Institutes in Wales established their own libraries, which proved a valuable means of helping people to practise the discipline of regular reading, but their emphasis tended to be on educational works which were, in general, in English. Miners' libraries may have been more effective than public libraries in meeting the needs of the population in industrial areas, although their stocks of Welsh books tended to be comparatively small. The libraries of chapels and Sunday schools provided Welsh books on religious and moral themes, and perhaps the existence of such a market tended to encourage publishers to continue to publish books of that kind.

At the turn of the twentieth century, the situation was transformed through the generosity of Andrew Carnegie, who built a number of local libraries for authorities who were willing to adopt the act, and its successor act of 1919. But the services provided by most of Wales's authorities were limited, and libraries did not consider that making Welsh books available was an important part of their responsibility. Many professional practitioners, reflecting the prevailing educational philosophy of the time, believed that the way forward lay with books in English. The growth of the Welsh public library service in the twentieth century was slow and uneven. By 1932, when Carmarthenshire adopted the public libraries acts (being the last Welsh local authority to do so), there was provision throughout Wales, though some libraries were functioning on a shoestring. In the mid-century, Welsh books did not form a high proportion of lending stock, no more than twenty per cent in areas where the proportion of Welsh speakers was significantly higher. But this situation also reflected the shortage of new Welsh books being published: until the 1960s it was still practical for an individual to buy every one which appeared.

By the time of the First World War, the Welsh book world was in crisis.

On the one hand the Census of 1911 had confirmed the existence of a million Welsh speakers (the highest number recorded), and the largest potential market for Welsh books. On the other, Welsh publishers suffered from a paucity of resources, distribution, and vision in that fast-changing age, factors which could be laid at the feet of the public as much as publishers. As the poet Sarnicol mocked:

> If you wish to please enlightened Welsh people, Talk to them about books; If you choose to frighten them, Talk to them about buying them.

The Welsh market declined as the Census of 1921 showed a reduction in the number of Welsh speakers. The population of Wales was also by then more thoroughly bilingual, and readers of the younger generation were turning to English-language works of literature, politics and philosophy which were unavailable in Welsh. The Great War brought publishers economic problems, such as losing staff to the armed forces, as well as substantial rises in the cost of paper and wages; inevitably, book prices followed suit. By 1921, the situation was so gloomy that Ifan ab Owen Edwards sought to recruit purchasers for Welsh books by establishing 'Urdd y Cyni' (the League of Distress), whose members would commit to buying one Welsh book per month throughout 1921. The League secured 557 members by April 1922, but had little long-term effect. During the years of the Depression, the situation of publishers remained fragile, and many Welsh people left their homeland, so reducing the market for Welsh books even further.

But the outlook was not entirely bleak. Influenced by the important report *Welsh in Education and Life* (1927), schools began to accord greater respect to Welsh as a subject, although growth was uneven until the establishment of Welsh-medium schools following the Second World War. The academic status accorded to the language in the University of Wales encouraged literary and bibliographic activity, and the establishment of the University of Wales Press in 1922 was a means of strengthening academic publishing in Welsh and English. An indication of the wish to broaden the horizons of Welsh by producing translations of European classics was the publication of Cyfres y Werin

(The People's Series) between 1919 and 1927; and Cyfres y Brifysgol a'r Werin (The University and People's Series) (1928–49) was an attempt to present the fruits of academic research to a general audience.

The publication of *Orgraff yr Iaith Gymraeg* (The Orthography of the Welsh Language) in 1928 confirmed a new standard for the written language. Even so, it was not easy for publishers to achieve sales; during the 1920s and 1930s, the number of new titles published each year hovered around the one hundred mark, and in a time of economic depression many simply could not afford to buy books. As so often in the history of the book in Welsh, it was the vision and enterprise of individuals which cut through difficulties. Prosser Rhys achieved considerable success from 1937 onwards with his Clwb Llyfrau Cymreig (Welsh Book Club), which attracted 3,000 subscribers. And when in 1940, the brothers Aneirin, Elfyn and Alun Talfan Davies established Llyfrau'r Dryw (Wren Books), a new vision of popular and reasonably priced books was fulfilled by authors who could appeal to a wide audience, such as W. Ambrose Bebb, R.T. Jenkins and E. Tegla Davies.

During the Second World War, when many social activities were curtailed, as during the pandemic of 2020–21, there was something of a renaissance in reading: in the 1940s and 1950s, Gwasg Gomer could expect to print 3,000 copies of each Welsh novel, and as many as 6,000 of *Chwalfa* (Upheaval) by T. Rowland Hughes, which appeared in 1946. 3,000 copies of *Cysgod y Cryman* (The Shadow of the Sickle) were printed for Christmas 1953, and a further 2,500 were needed in February 1954. But in the subsequent years of great social change, the industry was forced to wake up and be completely transformed by the establishment of a new regime of public funding.

One of the glories of the book is its durability. Although new media have been developed to transfer information and although texts may be clothed in computerised dress, the book remains a handy and portable artefact, much loved by many. It is striking that during the pandemic of 2020–21, the book trade suffered far less than many arts-based organisations, as in enforced seclusion, people turned to books for solace and entertainment, often discovering new areas of interest. The minister and writer Emrys ap Iwan believed that books would remain friends when other friends departed, yet it is doubtful whether Welsh people have ever fully taken seriously his exhortation to make 'friends of books'. Through the centuries, authors, printers and booksellers have struggled to ensure the continuation of the Welsh book, fighting against poverty and lack of resources as well as the frequent apathy of the market. It could be said that the Welsh have had an ambiguous relationship with their books from the start: glad to have them in their native tongue, but reluctant to give the support necessary for successful book production and distribution. Nevertheless, the book in Wales must surely be counted an important part of the miracle of the survival of the Welsh language. Had Welsh not become the language of print and of the Bible in the sixteenth century, had it not continued as a print language when a book trade was established in eighteenth-century Wales, it is doubtful whether it would have survived to be a language of learning and literature in our own time. It was the vision of humanists in the sixteenth century which saved Welsh for the modern world. Vision is needed in today's world of continual digital expansion, in order to celebrate anew the tenacity which has safeguarded both our language and the existence of Welsh books through the ages.

Rhidian Griffiths is editor of *Y Llyfr yng Nghymru / Welsh Books Studies* (1998) among other titles.
Translations are the author's own.

Laying the Foundations

*Welsh-language publishing
up to the seventies*

Laying the Foundations

Rheinallt Llwyd on Welsh-language
publishing up to the seventies

It is difficult – if not impossible – for anyone under fifty to comprehend the nature of the cultural landscape in Wales before the days of the Books Council of Wales. It is one of our acknowledged cultural institutions, and the object of admiration and frequently of amazement in countries which, like Wales, have minority languages and cultures. Yet this is a far cry from the state of publishing in Wales at the beginning of the 1950s, when the industry faced major difficulties. It is worth recalling the words of Islwyn Ffowc Elis an author who was starting his career at that time:

> There were about fifty Welsh-language books for adults being published in a year, and about the same for children. There were no grants to be had anywhere to publish a Welsh book or periodical, no Welsh Books Council, no Welsh Arts Council.[1]

And we could now add, no Welsh Academy or Literature Wales or Tŷ Newydd or Welsh Government, and so on. In a word, there was no public funding, and it was the handful of individual Welsh publishers who were wholly responsible for producing books, periodicals and other varied publications without any kind of financial support. The circumstances and regulations of the free market alone held sway.

But problems for publishers of Welsh-language books did not begin in 1950. What exacerbated the situation then was the spiralling of printing costs and a severe shortage of paper. The situation had been very different some seventy-five years previously, when there was an appetite for Welsh books and journals, so much so that the growth of printing and the book trade made for a flourishing local industry (Rhidian Griffiths describes elsewhere the emergence of the 'golden age of publishing in Wales'). This success was not to last and by the end of the first quarter of the twentieth century the book trade was in decline for a number of reasons.[2] By 1925, for instance, the sum total of Welsh-language books published had fallen to 74, from 155 in 1909.[3] The report *Welsh in Education and Life*, published in 1927, expressed grave concern: '[The] English daily paper, which reaches even the remotest parts of Wales, has proved almost too strong a rival for the Welsh weeklies, though its relation to the intellectual needs of the Welsh people is exiguous.' And the disappearance of the old book distributors, and the fact that each religious denomination had established its own bookroom to print, publish and distribute directly to its members, meant that it was more difficult to get hold of more 'secular' books. '[Throughout] the whole of Wales there are not more than ten booksellers' shops,' said the report, 'where a new Welsh book can be bought without inordinate trouble'.[4]

The report's analysis of the situation was clear and unequivocal, and the recommendations concerning books for school pupils showed clear vision. Translation boards should be established, to ensure that classic texts from English and other languages were available to the children of Wales; the University of Wales Press should direct and support authors in the production of Welsh books for children; much better provision should be made for libraries in schools and 'an exhibition of modern Welsh books, which could be circulated among the towns and villages of Wales, would be of considerable benefit to teachers of Welsh and would arouse interest on the part of the public'.[5] These were valuable suggestions which were not, unfortunately, acted upon. The recommendations concerning Welsh books for adults did not display the same vision, with a longing look back in the recommendation on the one hand that the National Union of Welsh Societies should 'endeavour to re-establish, if possible, the *dosbarthwr* (distributor), or to find some substitute', and on the other that an 'appeal for funds for the publication of Welsh books' should be organised.[6]

Nevertheless, the exceptional activity of the Union of Welsh Societies, established in 1913, and its varied efforts to promote interest in the reading and publication of Welsh books, should not be forgotten.[7] Numerous exhibitions were organised to give publicity to Welsh books and an idea mooted by O.M. Edwards at the end of the nineteenth century – that there should be a centre 'where it would be possible to get hold of all the most recent Welsh books'[8] – was resurrected. All this, of course, would depend on voluntary activity, and there were more urgent priorities in the depressed Wales of the late 1920s than promoting the Welsh book trade. Nevertheless, the report *Welsh in Education and Life* remains an important milestone in the history of publishing in Wales. It emphasised the fundamental problem of 'supply and demand' and the fact that 'the writing of books is mainly done by enthusiasts as a labour of love in leisure hours'.[9]

During the 1930s and 1940s it was only by the effort and sacrifice of individual publishers that the book trade was maintained without any public funding – and by the vision of a number of notable individuals, chief among whom was E. Prosser Rhys. A poet and journalist, he founded Gwasg Aberystwyth (The Aberystwyth Press) in 1928, partly in an attempt to fill the obvious gaps in Welsh publications for children, which had been noted in *Welsh in Education and Life*. He also undertook the publication of works by some of the most prominent Welsh authors of the time, such as Saunders Lewis, T.H. Parry-Williams, Kate Roberts, and two by the name of D.J. Williams, one from Fishguard and the other from Llandderfel. The first publication of this publisher in 1928 was the controversial poetic duo *Y Mynach a'r Sant: dwy awdl* by D. Gwenallt Jones, but when Gwenallt returned to Prosser Rhys ten years later, seeking a publisher for his first collection of poems, he was rejected. By the late 1930s, Gwenallt was one of Wales's most eminent poets as well as a recognised scholar. In 1968, not long before his death, he recounted the story in full on a audio tape preserved at the National Library of Wales:

> I asked [Prosser Rhys] to publish… *Ysgubau'r Awen*, but he refused. And he gave three reasons:… First, I didn't belong to any [religious] denomination. Second, the volume would never go to schools. If a volume went to schools, to the upper forms, of course, it would pay its way. Third, it was classical, that is, unpopular… Rhys was the editor of [the weekly newspaper] *Y Faner* and published books and knew more than anyone else about the tastes of readers of Welsh.[10]

Gwenallt eventually struck a deal with Dafydd Lewis of Gomer Press to publish the volume privately, and within three years, a thousand copies had been sold. '[Rhys] asked me whether he might publish the second edition, and I told him to go to the devil,'[11] was Gwenallt's reaction.

But if Prosser Rhys failed to predict the success of *Ysgubau'r Awen*, he succeeded remarkably with another of his schemes, the Clwb Llyfrau Cymreig (Welsh Book Club), founded in 1937. Rhys's venture was inspired by the success of the Left Book Club, established by Victor Gollancz in 1936, and in 1937, an announcement appeared in *Baner ac Amserau Cymru*:

> Before drawing up a definite plan we appeal for the names of those who are prepared to receive four half-crown books in a year – an outlay of ten shillings a year. The aim of the Club will be to ensure a public of not less than a thousand for books dealing with the national problems of Wales.[12]

The response was astounding as noted elsewhere by Rhidian Griffiths.

Yet by 1939, the outlook for the Welsh book trade was critical, with a fall in the number of books published and in the number of readers. Then in December 1940, the formation of Llyfrau'r Dryw (Wren Books) began a highly successful publishing venture which greatly influenced the Welsh book trade (as outlined elsewhere by Rhidian Griffiths).[13] These cheap books reached new readers and soon became indispensable to the Welsh National Committee for Providing Welsh Books to the Armed Forces, which in turn stimulated the book trade.

This healthier situation accounts for the astounding success of Ymgyrch Lyfrau'r Urdd, the books campaign organised by Urdd Gobaith Cymru (The Welsh League of Youth), between 1941 and 1946. It was first been organised around St David's Day in 1937, leading to the sale of over a thousand books. In 1965, responsibility for the campaign passed from the Urdd to the newly created Welsh Books Council. It is difficult to envisage what the condition of the Welsh book trade would have been without this imaginative step by the Urdd, because as the prime mover of the campaign, R.E. Griffith, claimed:

> Apart from authors, publishers and booksellers no-one had any concern for the book trade, and it could have gone into terminal

decline in the 1940s had not the Urdd seen an opportunity to
innovate and experiment voluntarily in the field, an opportunity
to create a new market among people who were remote from
bookshops, and to make the reading of Welsh a fashionable
and popular pursuit.[14]

Urdd Gobaith Cymru also organised conferences from 1943 to 1945 to discuss
the campaign and 'the sale of Welsh books in general'. It is interesting to note
that (although these represented our principal publishers) only seven firms
were represented, namely Hughes and Son, Gwasg Gee, Gwasg Aberystwyth,
Gwasg y Brython, University of Wales Press, Gwasg Gomer and Llyfrau'r Dryw.
Another important matter on the agenda of the first conference in 1943 was 'the
propriety of establishing a national centre to distribute Welsh books',[15] though
over twenty years were to elapse before that idea bore fruit.

But only two years passed before the realisation of another of the important
dreams of the founder of the Urdd, Ifan ab Owen Edwards, and its principal
organiser, R.E. Griffith: the establishment of a union of Welsh publishers and
booksellers, which happened in July 1945. Undeb Gwerthu a Chyhoeddi Llyfrau
Cymraeg (The Union for Selling and Publishing Welsh Books), which will be
referred to from here on as the Union of Welsh Publishers and Booksellers.

By the end of the 1940s, it became clear that the success of the bookselling
campaign had underlined the obvious weaknesses of the trade. Only a few new
titles were published every year and many of those only in limited print runs,
because of the rationing of paper, which continued well after the war had ended.
The extraordinary successes of 1943–45 had also exhausted old stocks held by
publishers, so that by this period, there was a shortage of books available for
sale. It is not surprising therefore that another movement, Undeb Cymru Fydd
(New Wales Union), founded in 1941, should be voicing genuine concerns about
the lack of suitable Welsh books, especially for school pupils.

In addition to the increasing costs of book production and the problem
of paper shortages, there was a dearth of manuscripts suitable for publication.
Welsh publishers could not attract new authors, and as a result, Prosser Rhys's
dream, the Welsh Book Club, was wound up in 1952:

Our intention as editors of *Y Clwb Llyfrau Cymraeg* was to publish serious and lighter books alternately, but our plan failed. We could not secure enough manuscripts to select from them books both weighty and entertaining, and it was also much easier to secure historical books than creative literature. There are not enough writers in Wales with leisure to write books for a Club. We received a promise of books from many people, but the promise was not honoured because they were too busy with committees and various movements in their spare time. We did not succeed in getting a single novel, and only one volume of short stories was received.[16]

Not only was there a shortage of authors, but by the early 1950s, it appears that the habit of buying and reading Welsh books was also in decline, at a time when (according to the 1951 Census) 714,686 or 28.9% of inhabitants were Welsh speakers. The situation was so desperate that some believed that the whole future of Welsh-language publishing was in doubt. There was despair on all sides – amid authors, publishers, booksellers (few as they were), teachers and parents. Books for children were in real crisis, as I explore below.

But then two significant developments occurred, both associated with individuals who played an important and unique role in the history of publishing in Wales: A.W. Ready and Alun R. Edwards.

The Union of Welsh Publishers and Booksellers, with R.E. Griffith as its energetic secretary, set to tackling the problems of the field in the early 1950s. Griffith, as Director of Urdd Gobaith Cymru and principal promoter of the Urdd Books Campaign, knew more than anyone about the state of the book trade. A memorandum was drawn up and submitted in June 1951 to the Council for Wales and Monmouthshire, the nominated body established by Clement Attlee's government in 1948 to consider Welsh-related matters and advise central government. The council had no powers, something which was a source of increasing frustration to its first chairman, Huw T. Edwards, a cultured Welshman who was Secretary of the Transport and General Workers' Union in north Wales, up to the time of his resignation in 1958. But in 1951, acutely aware as he was of the seriousness of the situation, Edwards acted immediately on receipt of the memorandum from the Union of Publishers and Booksellers. He sent the document to the Home Office and by the time of the National Eisteddfod at Llanrwst in August 1951, he could report to the Union that J. Chuter-Ede, the Home Secretary, was likely to appoint a small committee to look into the question.[17] Although Huw T. Edwards kept in close contact with the Home Office on the one hand and with the representative of the Union of Publishers and Booksellers on the other, the signs were not hopeful. As R.E. Griffith said:

> There was a definite feeling amongst the Publishers that the Government had not grasped the Welsh problem, notwithstanding the fact that we had so clearly stressed the matter in our Memorandum, and we also know that you based your case on our behalf on these national grounds. It is, of course, the old, old problem of trying to get the Government to appreciate that we are a distinct nation with a language and culture of our own. Ample reference is made in the enclosed minutes to the dissatisfaction we feel over this matter.[18]

The Home Office was, however, persuaded of the need to act, and on 20 October 1951, Chuter-Ede issued a warrant of appointment naming the members of a committee which was:

> To examine the present arrangements for the publication of books, magazines and periodicals in the Welsh language, and to report as to any measures which are desirable and practicable to meet the needs of Welsh schools and colleges and the Welsh-speaking population of Wales.[19]

The chairman of the committee would be A.W. Ready, an experienced publisher and director of the firm of G. Bell & Sons, and the other two members, Dr Ifor L. Evans, Principal of University College of Wales, Aberystwyth, and Goronwy Roberts, Member of Parliament for Caernarfonshire since 1945. J.E. Daniel, one of the inspectors of schools in the Welsh Department of the Ministry of Education, would act as secretary to the committee, an appointment which greatly pleased Huw T. Edwards. As he stated:

> I have expressed the view to [J.E. Daniel] that as far as the future of the Welsh language and the Welsh way of life is concerned, this Committee is the most important that has ever been set up and I

have suggested to him that the council itself might send
a deputation to support the claims of the publishers.[20]

Significantly, he added: 'I have also suggested that there should be set up a body to whom the Treasury may be able to make grants; this is in my view the only way to overcome the difficulty of subsidising.' Huw T. Edwards thought it would be a mistake to give too much responsibility for the publishing of children's books to the Welsh Joint Education Committee, 'for they would look upon the matter as a side-line rather than a main issue'. This prophecy was later fulfilled, at least in part.

While the 'Ready Committee', as it came to be called, was collecting evidence, R.E. Griffith was seeking an assurance, on behalf of the publishers, from the Ministry of Materials for more paper for printers in Wales, but in a letter to Huw T. Edwards in January 1952, he complains bitterly about the Ministry's attitude: 'The Publishers are very concerned indeed over the shabby treatment they have received from the Ministry of Materials.'[21] Although several months had passed since the publishers' request was submitted, the Ministry in London had not even acknowledged it.

Interesting also is the reference in this letter to a memorandum by the librarian of Cardiganshire suggesting 'the feasibility of establishing a National Publishing Trust in Wales'. And R.E. Griffith added: 'I will not enlarge upon this matter now, as you will probably be hearing direct from the Cardiganshire Education Authority.' We know that the Cardiganshire Education Authority was one of the bodies which submitted oral evidence to the Ready committee.

By the end of June 1952, the committee had completed its report and in a letter to Huw T. Edwards the chairman, A.W. Ready, maintains that it would be possible, by implementing the principal recommendations, to ease the problems of Welsh-language publishing quite significantly, especially in the field of books for children. But he also notes possible obstacles in terms of the matter falling between various ministries and governmental departments. Such fears continued into the changing of guards, from Chuter-Ede to Sir David Maxwell Fyfe, who became both Home Secretary and Minister for Welsh Affairs.

During the summer months of 1952, considerable pressure was brought to bear to ensure that when the Ready report appeared, its recommendations would be acted upon. Huw T. Edwards wrote to Sir David, noting that the Ready committee 'have recommended the only successful approach to what is a very difficult problem, i.e. the setting-up of a Welsh Books Foundation'.[22] Huw T., with his confident enthusiasm, firmly believed that it would be possible to attract the support of Welsh local authorities and that of many Welsh exiles, outside Wales and across the Atlantic, for the idea. The main thrust of his letter to the Home Secretary was that the government of the day should give a strong lead and show the extent of its goodwill by putting the Foundation on a firm financial footing, with £125,000, to cover the first five years.

Although the Ready report is now forgotten, it is in fact an important milestone in the history of Welsh-language publishing. This was the first time ever that central government gave detailed consideration both to the book trade in Wales and to the idea of public funding for its publishing industry. The economic and cultural reasons for concern over the future of the publishing industry are analysed, and a clear statement given of the importance of print culture for the nation's life. And despite the technological developments of recent decades, the central importance of print culture remains:

> Books are an indispensable means to the preservation, continuity, and development of a national culture. A bookless people is a rootless people, doomed to lose its identity, and its power of contributing to the common fund of civilisation.... If the published language goes, the language itself as a cultural medium will soon follow: and if Welsh goes, a bastardised vernacular will take its place, lacking both pride of ancestry and hope of posterity.[23]

The report notes that it was a task for 'the nation as a whole' to ensure that the Welsh-language publishing industry flourished, and it was therefore appropriate that a central national organisation should bring this about. The report's principal recommendation was the establishment of 'a Welsh Books Foundation... primarily for the supply, to Local Authorities, of Welsh books for the use of schools, but with power, under certain circumstances to stimulate the general provision of Welsh books'.[24] Around £40,000 per annum would be needed to support the Foundation in its first five years, the income '[to] be derived partly from local government and partly from central government sources… Each Local Authority should be able, at its discretion, to contribute either out of the rates or out of the income of its Tithe Money'.[25]

Urging the principle that a direct subsidy could be available from central government for the publication of Welsh books, especially those aimed at schools, was an important step in the history of publishing in Welsh, and this was certainly the most important contribution made by the Ready report. It is also interesting, if only from a historical standpoint, to note some of the other recommendations in the report which received little attention or discussion at the time. From time to time, said the report, the National Library of Wales and the Welsh Library Association should be asked to organise a 'National Welsh Books Exhibition' and ensure more general publicity of the nature of 'Read Welsh Books'. And for the first time in an official government report, the idea of establishing 'a central clearing-house for all Welsh books'[26] was mooted.

The Ready Committee was quite certain of the way in which the Welsh Books Foundation should be established and administered. The Welsh Joint Education Committee should 'provide the necessary rooms' and, along with the University Education Department and the Council for Wales and Monmouthshire, should have representatives on the small body which would administer the Foundation. The Foundation would also have members chosen by the Minister of Education and the Minister for Welsh Affairs. There would be no-one representing Welsh publishers or any other part of the book trade. Most important of all was that the Ready report rejected one of the main recommendations in the memorandum sent to the Home Secretary in June 1951: 'The possibility of a direct subsidy to the publishers, as suggested in the original memorandum of the Union was immediately rejected, as involving a dangerous and impracticable principle.'[27]

Every attempt was made to gain maximum publicity for the *Report of the Committee on Welsh-Language Publishing* on its appearance in October 1952. The Honourable Society of Cymmrodorion, along with the Council for Wales and Monmouthshire and the Welsh Joint Education Committee, organised a day conference held at Llandrindod, at which the principal guest speaker, Sir Emrys

Evans (Principal of the University College of North Wales, Bangor) gave an inspiring speech:

> Sir Emrys spoke of the vitamins of Welsh life and culture, the life-giving elements which depended on nurture and succour if the nation was to live. It was Welsh books and literature which would accomplish that. Without them, the language, which is 1,500 years old, would disappear. It would not be her fate, he said, to die quietly in a single night, but to suffer the agonies of a slow death over many years, and that was much worse.[28]

The Principal went on to list the alien influences which threatened Welshness, insisting that what was needed in face of the crisis was 'to publish more Welsh books for schools and ensure that there was a market for them.'

There was considerable unanimity at the conference for supporting the main recommendations of the Ready report. But others regarded them as inadequate. A week before the Llandrindod conference, some Cardiganshire teachers discussed the report at a weekend conference near Newcastle Emlyn. A number of resolutions were passed there, all proposing amendments. Evidently, the greatest fear was that the Welsh Books Foundation recommended by Ready would fall into the hands of bureaucrats who would not necessarily have a proper understanding of the situation. It was therefore important:

1. That we as a conference give our approval to this report as far as it goes.

2. That the Foundation Committee should include members whose knowledge of Welsh books is extensive and whose interest in the language and culture of Wales is profound.

3. That the Welsh Books Foundation should be established in April 1953 – at the beginning of the financial year.

4. That an experienced person is needed to administer the scheme.

5. That we appeal to Cardiganshire to give a lead to the other Authorities by contributing the whole of the penny rate and also any other sum suggested from the tithe money.[29]

Present at the conference was the county librarian, Alun R. Edwards, who also subsequently expressed concerns to Huw T. Edwards that the report neglected the reading needs of adults in favour of those of schoolchildren. But Alun R. Edwards was not the only one to express disappointment. In January 1953, another memorandum was drawn up on behalf of the Union of Welsh Publishers and Booksellers, expressing general support for the Ready recommendations but voicing concern that too little attention had been paid in the report to the interests of Wales's booksellers, and also echoing Edwards's warning about the balance between educational and general books. The secretary of the Council for Wales and Monmouthshire, J.L. Palmer, privately held a similar view, and was also concerned that the proposed Foundation become stranded as a conceptual plaything within the Ministry of Education's brief.

Unfortunately, Palmer's fears were realised. Sir Ben Bowen Thomas, Principal of the Welsh Division of the Education Ministry, suggested, around this same time, that during its first five years, the Foundation's main thrust should be to concentrate on producing books for schools through the body already in existence, the Welsh Joint Education Committee. And that is what happened: virtually all efforts following the publication of the Ready report were directed to fulfilling the need for Welsh books for schools. No mention was made of subsidies for books for adults until 1956, when the central government decided to make a grant of £1,000 to Welsh publishers, to be distributed by the University of Wales Press.[30]

And yet it is the case, as mentioned above, that the field of Welsh-language books for children had been in crisis for some time. Alun R. Edwards, that energetic thirty-year-old librarian of Cardiganshire – and the youngest British county librarian at that time – had been grappling with these and other problems of the Welsh book trade, in his own way. Alun would emerge as one of the most innovative public librarians in Wales during the 1950s and 1960s, and the principal benefactor of our country's book publishing industry.[31]

Early in 1950, the Cardiganshire schools' librarian returned to Aberystwyth one afternoon with a stern message from the headmistress of Swyddffynnon Primary School, near Tregaron: 'Tell Alun Edwards, if he's going to continue to pour English books over schoolchildren he's going to kill the Welsh language.'[32] Her words came as a considerable shock, so much so that, for the rest of that year, Edwards spent much of his time trying to persuade certain English publishers of children's books to consent to translations or Welsh adaptations of their publications. He did achieve considerable success with Collins, because around twenty Welsh titles appeared in time, most of them adapted by John Eilian (John Tudor Jones, journalist, broadcaster, translator and both chaired and crowned bard). It is worth recalling that the percentage of Welsh speakers in Cardiganshire in the early 1950s was 79.5% (according to the 1951 Census) and that 7.4% were monoglot Welsh speakers. And yet, only thirteen Welsh books for children appeared in 1950.

A shortage of Welsh books for children was not the only problem. When writing his first annual report, the county librarian realised that the number of loans of English books to adults was rising rapidly whereas loans of Welsh books to adults were in decline. And the obvious reason for this was that there were so few titles available. In 1950, there appeared an additional 87 books for adults, making a total of 100. Of these, seventeen were of a religious nature and sixteen were plays. Only six novels appeared during the year.[33] Before the end of that year, Alun Edwards had come up with the idea (which apparently he aired on a radio programme) of establishing an independent national body, a 'National Publishing Trust', to which all county councils in Wales would contribute in order to promote publishing in the Welsh language. And that was the precise structure adopted for the foundation of the Welsh Books Council in 1961. Ironically, considering the commissions coming his way that Edwards had inspired, John Eilian was vigorously opposed to the idea, and referred to Alun R. Edwards as 'the unsleeping County Librarian of Cardiganshire'.[34]

But the dream of establishing a national body was a long-term one. In the meantime, local action was necessary. And that is what happened, with the aim not only of increasing the number of Welsh books for children and enabling local publishing, but also of nurturing authors, as well as supporting all sorts of plans to promote the book trade generally. In July 1951, a month after R.E. Griffith's memorandum on the plight of the Welsh-language book trade had been submitted to the Council for Wales and Monmouthshire, a Welsh Books Committee was established as one of the sub-committees of the Cardiganshire Education Committee, with a recommendation that £2,000 should be spent on promoting the writing, illustrating and publishing of books for children. A problem arose, however, when the Ministry of Education decreed that such a step was unlawful. The Education Authority was quite at liberty to purchase books which already existed, but not to publish new ones! The county was, however, given the right to produce and publish books which were wholly local in character 'and of use to the schools of the county', provided they were not sold on the open market.

In response to this challenge Alun Edwards immediately began to organise residential weekend courses to train budding authors, and a special conference was held, once again, near Newcastle Emlyn, not far from the spot where Isaac Carter had established the first printing press in Wales in 1718. In late September 1952, 48 of the county's teachers assembled there, among them people like T. Llew Jones who were to become eminent authors. From that conference emerged innovative volumes such as *Atlas Ceredigion*, *Detholiad o Bant a Bryn*, *Cerddi Gwlad ac Ysgol* and *Cen Ceredigion*. A publisher was found for each manuscript accepted, and the Education Authority undertook to purchase between 500 and 1000 copies. This was the beginning of a pioneering scheme, generously supported by the Director and Education Committee of Cardiganshire. In time, the counties of Merioneth and Caernarfon were persuaded to join the scheme to purchase popular books for children. Other counties became part of the venture; three counties grew to five, and five to seven, until the whole was eventually made over to the Welsh Joint Education Committee as a national scheme.[35]

A similar story can be told in the context of Welsh books for adults, namely action at a local level as a prelude to activity at national level. After the disappointment of the Ready report, efforts were made to establish Cymdeithas Lyfrau Ceredigion (The Cardiganshire Book Society), and to attract members by a kind of subscription scheme, in which everyone bought book tokens valued at two guineas and exchanged them in bookshops. But this society developed into a publishing house as well, and Professor Dafydd Jenkins gives a detailed account of how, at the end of 1954, this was achieved by inducing Cardiganshire County Council to grant an interest-free loan of £5,000 from the Tithe Fund, and an annual grant of £1,000 under the Local Government Act of 1948, to support the society's publishing programme.[36] This company remained active in publishing for around fifty-five years. Many of the early titles were books of reminiscences, some of them the outcome of competitions organised by the Book Society. Cardiganshire Library also undertook the organisation of a programme of cultural activities such as Welsh book quizzes for children, young people and adults, and a network of book discussion groups, all to foster renewed interest in reading and the promotion of the book trade.

It was not only in Cardiganshire that book societies were active by the mid-1950s. A group of patriotic Welsh people in London had established Clwb Llyfrau Llundain (The London Book Club) on 1 May 1953, a year and more before Cymdeithas Lyfrau Ceredigion was even heard of, and it proved a most successful experiment.[37] Other Welsh counties followed the pattern set by Cardiganshire, as county societies multiplied from the mid-1950s onward, as related by Alun R. Edwards's volume, *Yr Hedyn Mwstard*.[38] Thomas Parry, then National Librarian, and Alun R. Edwards spent many evenings travelling the length and breadth of Wales, encouraging people to form county societies. The Union of Welsh Book Societies was eventually formed and *Noddwr Llyfrau Cymraeg* (The Welsh Book Patron) was published from 1958 to 1964.

It was the Union which in the end gave rise to the Books Council, established in November 1961. Until the first director, Alun Creunant Davies, began work on 1 March 1965, it was the Cardiganshire librarian and his staff who were responsible for nurturing the new organisation, although Edwards was assisted by Enid Roberts (now Canon Enid Morgan) from January 1964; she edited the first issue of *Llais Llyfrau/Book News from Wales*, which came out that summer.

It was not only within Wales that Alun R. Edwards was promoting the cause of the Welsh book trade. When, in September 1957, the Ministry of Education established a committee to study the structure and services of public libraries in England and Wales, the librarian of Cardiganshire presented evidence on behalf of the Cardiganshire and Aberystwyth Joint Library, drawing attention to the unique needs of Wales. The resulting report (the Roberts Report), published in February 1959 did in fact dedicate a whole chapter to Wales. The importance of the Welsh language and culture for the 'substantial minority' who speak it is underlined, and the huge problem 'of satisfying demands for books in Welsh' emphasised. The report also notes the need to increase interest in Welsh books and ensure that Wales has suitable librarians to serve her bilingual communities: people well versed in the language, history and literature of the country. It was this important report which also recommended that a library school, providing full-time courses, should be established in Wales;[39] by October 1964, the College of Librarianship Wales had been established near Aberystwyth.

Following the publication of this report, the Department of Education and Science established, in March 1961, a working party to look at the standards of service in public libraries in England and Wales; the only Welsh representative on that committee was Alun R. Edwards. The resulting Bourdillon report, *Standards of Public Library Service in England and Wales*, appearing in December 1962, also contained a chapter dedicated to Wales, where emphasis is placed on the need to give appropriate and equal service to Welsh speakers. Indeed, the Bourdillon report has the following among its recommendations:

> Public libraries in Wales have a comparable responsibility for
> stimulating interest in and demand for Welsh language books as
> for English books but to achieve anything approaching comparability
> with the service of library material in English it would be necessary
> considerably to increase the number of titles issued annually in Welsh.[40]

Another recommendation made by the working party was that public library authorities in Wales should devise a scheme to justify publishing any Welsh book suitable for borrowing from a public library. According to the librarian of Cardiganshire, however, the final recommendations of the report did not go far enough, as he was in favour of creating The Public Libraries Welsh Books Fund in order to ensure the purchase of 500 copies of every book appropriate for schools and public libraries. Though he failed to persuade the other members of the working party, his detailed proposals were published in a most revealing statement within the final report, entitled 'Reservations by Mr Alun R. Edwards with regard to the position in Wales'.[41]

Certainly, the publication of the Bourdillon report so soon after the establishment of the Books Council was a crucial step, and the reference in the report to 'purchasing 500 copies of every appropriate book' was an incentive to the Books Council in its early days.[42] The Council would not have grown at all during the 1960s, but for the essential support of Wales's libraries, and, as is noted elsewhere here, it was their particular needs which the Council met at that time.

It was during the decade 1951–61, when the Conservative governments of Churchill, Eden and Macmillan were in power, that the foundations were laid for the body which would eventually grow to be an essential national institution in Wales. It is plain that the Books Council literally appeared, as though book-ended, between the 1952 Ready report and the 1962 Bourdillon report. But the work of committees and government was inspired and spurred on by certain energetic, determined individuals, often giving up their own free time to secure the dream of a professional footing for Welsh-language books for Wales.

Some historians have argued that 'the 1950s were a depressing decade for language campaigners',[43] if one were to consider the Council's emergence against the backdrop of national consciousness. It is true that there are ad hoc, almost serendipitous elements in the run-up to the Council's establishment, not least the fact that it was a minister in Clement Attlee's government who was responsible for establishing the Ready committee at a time when Wales had no voice in the cabinet of central government in London.

But from the early 1960s, the campaign for the language became a fiery political battle, the year 1962 alone seeing the broadcast of Saunders Lewis's lecture, *Tynged yr Iaith* (The Fate of the Language) and the establishment of Cymdeithas yr Iaith (The Welsh Language Society). So, at the very time when the new-born body, the Welsh Books Council, was fighting for its life, there began a period of incomparable activity in campaigning for the survival of the language itself.

The Books Council developed in parallel with a growth in national consciousness and campaigning to achieve a stronger identity and greater self-government for the nation. It is within Wales that the fight for the future of the publishing industry and the book trade is now fought. Many of the early leaders of the language movement have become prominent and influential figures in the book trade as printers and publishers, authors and founders of bookshops throughout Wales. At one time, there was controversy in the columns of *Tafod y Ddraig* (The Dragon's Tongue), the journal of the Welsh Language Society, as to whether it was the duty of budding Welsh-speaking authors and poets to write, or to use their talents and energies to be politically active in the cause of the language.

Meanwhile, action continued at traditional, institutional level. In November 1963, the Council for Wales and Monmouthshire published its *Report on the Welsh Language Today*,[44] in which a whole section is assigned to publishing, and which contains a number of specific recommendations. The recommendations welcome the establishment of the Welsh Books Council but also stress 'the special difficulties inevitably associated with this limited market [publishing Welsh books for adults] and the continually rising costs of production. We are concerned lest the withdrawal of Government financial help after 1965 will place the publication of these books once again in jeopardy'.[45] The central government grant did not, as was once feared, come to an end in 1965, and it remained an essential means of support for Welsh publishers for years afterwards.

The year 1967 saw an exceptionally important development in the cultural context, and one which proved the salvation of the fragile Welsh Books Council, which had no hope of meaningful expansion with only its income from local authorities and support from publishers to rely on. This was the year of the foundation of the Welsh Arts Council, in succession to the Welsh Committee of the Arts Council of Great Britain, and of the appointment of a number of artform directors. The appointment of the energetic Meic Stephens to head the Literature Section led to this section becoming the main source of subsidy for Welsh authors and publishers (in both languages), given that the income of the Welsh Arts Council was so much greater than that of other funders.[46]

While financial subsidies were on the increase during the early 1970s, there were other developments which would accrue to the advantage of the book trade, most of them the result of goodwill and voluntary action by lovers of Welsh language and literature. From 1973 onward, a network of community newspapers was developed in every part of the country, reaching many people who were not in the habit of reading books in Welsh.[47] And the second half of the 1970s saw the establishment of societies which operated wholly in Welsh; it was from one of these, Cymdeithas Cerdd Dafod, that Cyhoeddiadau Barddas emerged as a publishing house of quality and influence. It was in 1978 also that the Council for the Welsh Language published its report, *Cyhoeddi yn yr Iaith Gymraeg/Publishing in the Welsh Language*, which emphasised some of the developments seen since the early 1960s and stressed the danger of over-dependence on grants.[48]

Meanwhile, there had been significant developments in the world of broadcasting, such as the establishment of Radio Cymru in 1977 and Radio Wales in 1978, and numerous changes in the world of television from the time of Teledu Cymru, at the beginning of the 1960s, up to the foundation of S4C in 1982. All these changes impacted directly or indirectly on the world of publishing, because of the growing need for writers for radio and television alike. Over a period of thirty years and more, there have been notable examples of authors, such as Eigra Lewis Roberts, Manon Rhys and Wiliam Owen Roberts, who have contributed extensively to the media and to traditional authorship.[49] But there was inevitably a huge difference in the level of income enjoyed by those who wrote for the media as opposed to traditional authors, as explained in the report *Y Fasnach Lyfrau yng Nghymru* (The Book Trade in Wales) in 1988.[50] One of the major problems which Griffith John Williams and Gwenallt faced as they wound up the Welsh Book Club in 1952 – that is the lack of resources for would-be fulltime writers – had been resolved, at least in part.

Since 1965, information technology and the computer revolution have influenced the progress of the book trade in Wales, as elsewhere. Technological developments have eased the work of every part of the book trade, from the individual author to those who distribute and sell the final product. By the mid-1960s, offset litho printing was rapidly gaining ground and was immediately adopted by Robat Gruffudd, the printer and publisher of the new Y Lolfa press, and by more established publishers like Gomer.[51] Above all else, developments in the production of books and other printed materials throughout the years of growth of the Books Council have been nothing less than revolutionary, and have benefited everyone in the industry, including authors, editors, designers and printers. From time to time, of course, the argument over the inherent value of print culture would re-emerge and there would be firm declarations in favour of 'visual literature' (*llunyddiaeth*) at the expense of traditional print literature alone. Some observers have indeed maintained that the days of the printed book are numbered; witness the following quotation:

> One of the most startling features of the Computer Revolution is that print and paper technology will appear as primitive as the pre-Caxtonian hand-copying of manuscripts seems to us. In sum, the 1980s will see the book as we know it, and as our ancestors created and cherished it, begin a slow but steady slide into oblivion.[52]

Of the numerous prophecies made by Christopher Evans regarding the impact of the microchip revolution on society, this is the only one to have been proved totally wrong. And although we are now in the midst of an extraordinary revolution in digital and electronic communication, print culture is holding its own remarkably well, partly because of the advantages which have flowed from technological developments. Meanwhile, let us rejoice in the contribution of the book trade to our lives and hopefully maintain, like the Ready report, that 'a bookless people is a rootless people'.

Rheinallt Llwyd is the editor of *Gwarchod y Gwreiddiau: Cyfrol Goffa Alun R. Edwards* (Protecting the Roots: In Memory of Alun R. Edwards) (1996) and joint editor (with Dr D. Huw Owen) of *Olrhain Hanes Bro a Theulu* (Tracing Community and Family History) (2009) and the revised and extended English version, *Searching for Family and Community History in Wales* (2014). He is also the author of the monograph, *Bro a Bywyd: Islwyn Ffowc Elis* (2007).

Notes

[1] Islwyn Ffowc Elis, 'Doedd neb yn ddiogel rhagddo', in Rheinallt Llwyd (ed.), *Gwarchod y Gwreiddiau* (Llandysul, Gwasg Gomer, 1996), p. 12 (translated by Rhidian Griffiths).

[2] Gwilym Huws, 'Welsh-language publishing 1919–1995', in Philip Henry Jones and Eiluned Rees (eds), *A Nation and its Books: A History of the Book in Wales* (Aberystwyth, National Library of Wales in association with Aberystwyth Centre for the Book, 1998), pp. 341–2.

[3] *Cylchgrawn Llyfrgell Genedlaethol Cymru / The National Library of Wales Journal*, XIII (1963–64), 306.

[4] *Welsh in Education and Life* (London, HMSO, 1927), pp. 178–9.

[5] Ibid., pp. 154–5.

[6] Ibid., p. 313.

[7] Marion Löffler, 'Mudiad yr Iaith Gymraeg yn Hanner Cyntaf yr Ugeinfed Ganrif: Cyfraniad y Chwyldroadau Tawel', in Geraint H. Jenkins and Mari A. Williams (eds), *'Eu Hiaith a Gadwant'?* (Caerdydd, Gwasg Prifysgol Cymru, 2000), pp. 192–4.

[8] Ibid., p. 193.

[9] *Welsh in Education and Life*, p. 160.

[10] John Lewis, *Creu Argraff: Atgofion Teulu Gwasg Gomer* (Llandysul, Gwasg Gomer, 2012), p. 97.

[11] Ibid., p. 98.

[12] E. Prosser Rhys, 'Ledled Cymru', *Baner ac Amserau Cymru*, 9 Mawrth 1937.

[13] Gwilym Huws, 'Llyfrau'r Dryw', *Llais Llyfrau*, Gaeaf 1990, 4–5.

[14] R.E. Griffith, *Urdd Gobaith Cymru: Cyfrol 1, 1922–1945* (Aberystwyth, Urdd Gobaith Cymru, 1971), p. 227.

[15] Ibid., p. 316.

[16] Circular dated April 1952, drawn up by Griffith John Williams and Gwenallt, see David Jenkins, 'Braslun o Hanes Argraffu yn Sir Aberteifi', *Journal of the Welsh Bibliographical Society*, VII (1950–53), 189; Rhisiart Hincks, *E. Prosser Rhys, 1901–1945* (Llandysul, Gwasg Gomer, 1980), p. 181.

[17] I am particularly grateful to one of Huw T. Edwards's granddaughters, Mrs Eleri Huws, Pont-y-clun, for permission to use a collection of documents (chiefly letters) in her possession. They are referred to from here on as the Huw T. Edwards Collection.

[18] Huw T. Edwards Collection, Letter from R.E. Griffith to Huw T. Edwards, 5 September 1951.

[19] Home Office, *Report of the Committee on Welsh Language Publishing* (London, HMSO, 1952), p. 1.

[20] Huw T. Edwards Collection, Letter from Huw T. Edwards to R.E. Griffith, 10 November 1951.

[21] Ibid. Letter from R.E. Griffith to Huw T. Edwards, 29 January 1952.

[22] Ibid. Letter from Huw T. Edwards to David Maxwell Fyfe, 4 July 1952.

[23] *Report of the Committee on Welsh Language Publishing*, pp. 2–3 (par. 11 and 12).

[24] Ibid., p. 10 (par. 46 a).

[25] Ibid., p. 10 (par. 46 b).

[26] Ibid., p. 10 (par. 47 c).

[27] Ibid., p. 5 (par. 24).

[28] *Y Cymro*, 28 November 1952.

[29] Huw T. Edwards Collection, Pwyllgor Addysg Sir Aberteifi, 'Penderfyniadau Athrawon Sir Aberteifi (Plas y Cilgwyn)', 14–15 November 1952.

[30] Council for Wales and Monmouthshire, *Report on the Welsh Language Today* (London, HMSO, 1963), p. 63.

[31] See Alun R. Edwards, *Yr Hedyn Mwstard: Atgofion Alun R. Edwards* (Llandysul, Gwasg Gomer, 1980); Rheinallt Llwyd (ed.), *Gwarchod y Gwreiddiau* (Llandysul, Gwasg Gomer, 1996); Rheinallt Llwyd, 'Alun R. Edwards: arloeswr a gwireddwr breuddwydion', *Ceredigion*, XV(1) (2005), 139–68.

[32] *Y Faner*, 25 April 1980, 12; *Yr Hedyn Mwstard*, p. 51.

[33] *Cylchgrawn Llyfrgell Genedlaethol Cymru / The National Library of Wales Journal*, XIII (1963–64), 306.

[34] John Eilian, 'Remedy could be worse than the disease', *Herald of Wales*, 23 February 1952, 3; *Yr Hedyn Mwstard*, p. 49.

[35] *Yr Hedyn Mwstard*, pp. 51–63.

[36] Dafydd Jenkins, 'Cymdeithas Lyfrau Ceredigion: Babi Alun Edwards', *Gwarchod y Gwreiddiau*, pp. 45–60.

[37] Emlyn Evans, *O'r Niwl a'r Anialwch* (Dinbych, 1991), pp. 207–9.

[38] *Yr Hedyn Mwstard*, pp. 70–7.

[39] Ministry of Education, *The Structure of the Public Library Service in England and Wales* (London, HMSO, 1959), pp. 23–5.

[40] Department of Education and Science, *Standards of Public Library Service in England and Wales* (London, HMSO, 1962), p. 51.

[41] Ibid., pp. 61–2. Alun R. Edwards's side of the story is recounted in *Yr Hedyn Mwstard*, pp. 103–17.

[42] *Yr Hedyn Mwstard*, p. 116.

[43] Geraint H. Jenkins a Mari A. Williams, 'Hynt yr iaith Gymraeg 1900–2000: Rhagymadrodd', *'Eu Hiaith a Gadwant'?*, p. 13.

[44] *Report on the Welsh Language Today*, pp. 147 (par. 365, 366).

[45] Ibid., p. 147.

[46] Tony Bianchi, *A review of the Literature Committee's work* (Cardiff: Welsh Arts Council, 1983); R. Brinley Jones, 'Gweithgarwch a chyfraniad Adran Lenyddiaeth Cyngor Celfyddydau Cymru', in *Gwarchod y Gwreiddiau*, pp. 130–44; Meic Stephens, *Hunangofiant Meic Stephens: Cofnodion* (Tal-y-bont, Y Lolfa, 2012), pp. 87–133.

[47] Gwilym Huws, 'Mwy na phapur newydd', *Gwarchod y Gwreiddiau*, pp. 215–36.

[48] Cyngor yr Iaith Gymraeg, *Cyhoeddi yn yr Iaith Gymraeg* (Cardiff, HMSO, 1978).

[49] Eigra Lewis Roberts, 'Ha' Bach/Minafon', *Llais Llyfrau*, Spring 1985, 4–5.

[50] Gweithgor yr Ymchwil Farchnad, *Y Fasnach Lyfrau yng Nghymru* (Aberystwyth, 1988), pp. 122–53, 261–2.

[51] John Lewis, *Creu Argraff*, pp. 135–40.

[52] Christopher Evans, *The Mighty Micro: The Impact of the Micro-chip Revolution* (Sevenoaks, Hodder and Stoughton/Coronet Books, 1980), pp. 104–5. [Originally published in 1979.]

The Growth of
the Mustard Seed

From the sixties to 2010

The Growth of
the Mustard Seed

Gwerfyl Pierce Jones on the sixties to 2010

It was not without some effort that the Welsh Books Council came into being in the early 1960s. Its creation was the culmination of years of tireless campaigning by a small number of ardent supporters of the Welsh language. By the mid-century publishing in Welsh was in a sorry state. There was a shortage of books and authors, not to mention competent editors, and the printing industry faced severe problems as paper costs had gone sky high and supplies were short.[1] The Union of Welsh Publishers and Booksellers (which came into being in 1943) appealed to the Council for Wales and Monmouthshire for assistance, and the chairman, Huw T. Edwards, played a key role in persuading the government of the day to set up a committee, chaired by the experienced publisher A.W. Ready, to review the state of affairs and submit recommendations to the government.[2] The story is fully told in Rheinallt Llwyd's contribution to this volume.

Despite its importance in the history of publishing in Welsh, many people thought the report of the Ready committee, completed in October 1952, rather disappointing, as it concentrated almost exclusively on children's books. It is also interesting to note that the report closed the door on the industry's request for direct financial aid 'as involving a dangerous and impracticable principle'.[3]

Probably one of the main contributions of the Ready committee was to draw the attention of a wider circle of people to the dire state of Welsh-language publishing and to ignite the enthusiasm of supporters to begin taking action to improve the situation. An instance of such action was the conference organised by the Cymmrodorion Society, with the co-operation of the Council for Wales and Monmouthshire, at Llandrindod in November 1952, when several passionate addresses were delivered by influential people such as D. Emrys Evans, the Principal of the University College of North Wales, Bangor. The occasion was widely reported in the press and many were inspired to act.

One of these was Emlyn Evans, the former director of Gwasg Gee, who was working in London at the time. It was his efforts which led to the foundation of a Welsh Book Society among the London Welsh; his energy secured a membership of over five hundred within a short time, and there were moves to establish branches in Birmingham and Liverpool.

The story of the celebrated meeting between Islwyn Ffowc Elis (already a promising young author), Dafydd Orwig (at the time a teacher in Blaenau Ffestiniog) and Emlyn Evans is recorded in the memorial volume to Dafydd Orwig and in the autobiography of Emlyn Evans and elsewhere.[4] It was the week following the National Eisteddfod at Ystradgynlais in 1954, and the three young men were on holiday in north Wales. After meeting for lunch in Dolgellau, they went for a spin in Islwyn's car (the famous A40, KLV 108), but stopped before reaching the Cross Foxes pub not far from the town and spent the next three hours discussing possibilities. The three were so concerned about the situation of Welsh books that they even considered giving up their jobs and 'chancing it in the fragile and uncertain world of producing and selling Welsh books'.[5] But that was a pipe dream, as not one of them had the accumulated capital with which to start a publishing venture. A more practical idea, therefore, was the possibility of establishing a network of Welsh book societies throughout Wales.

Within six months, by New Year's Day 1955, a conference had been organised at the offices of Urdd Gobaith Cymru in Aberystwyth, to discuss the matter. Dr Thomas Parry, at that time Librarian of the National Library of Wales, had accepted the invitation to chair the conference, and R. E. Griffith, the head of the Urdd and one of the leading figures in the Union of Publishers and Booksellers, and Alun R. Edwards, the innovative librarian of Cardiganshire, played a prominent part in the proceedings.[6] At this meeting R. E. Griffith formally proposed that a book society be established in every county in Wales and in some of the principal towns, with the option of adopting the structure of Cymdeithas Lyfrau Ceredigion (the Cardiganshire Book Society), which had been in existence for around two years and which operated by selling stamps to the public to be exchanged in bookshops; or that of Cymdeithas Lyfrau Llundain (the London Book Society), where a committee selected a book every two or three months and sent it by post to all members. Within a year, around fifteen societies had been established across the country, and a national association, Undeb Cymdeithasau Llyfrau Cymraeg dros Gymru a Lloegr (the Union of Welsh Book Societies in Wales and England), had been formed, with Thomas Parry as Honorary President. One of the most active of these was Cymdeithas Lyfrau Sir Gaernarfon (the Caernarfonshire Book Society), with Dafydd Orwig working assiduously to ensure that it fulfilled its promise.

While all this was going on, Alun Edwards was performing miracles in Cardiganshire.[7] If the Ready committee could not offer answers at a national level, he was determined to find answers locally. In his own inimitable way, he persuaded the County Council to spend £2,000 on purchasing Welsh books; managed to secure £1,000 to promote writing in Welsh; arranged for courses for writers to be held regularly; and played a key role in the foundation of Cymdeithas Lyfrau Ceredigion and in getting a loan of £5,000 from the County Council (which was later commuted to a gift). The way in which he did all this in the teeth of substantial opposition is extraordinary. Once Alun Edwards had set his heart on accomplishing any task, no possibility of failure could be countenanced. His energy was boundless, he boasted innumerable contacts, and had both a remarkable gift for persuasion and unyielding determination.

It was above all his exertions which led to the establishment of a national body to take responsibility for Welsh books, though many others contributed to the development. The need for a national body had been expressed in many quarters, but it is interesting to note that Alun Edwards had mooted the idea in a radio talk as early as 1950.[8] Even so, achieving the goal took years of conferences, committees and sub-committees, which is perhaps why there is not complete agreement over the year in which the Books Council was established. Although a conference was held in Cardiff in May 1959 (with the crucial support of Llewellyn Heycock, a powerful local government leader in Glamorgan), and the new body met for the first time in Shrewsbury in April 1960, the final meeting of the Union of Welsh Book Societies was held on 6 November 1961, which is the date normally cited as marking the establishment of the Welsh Books Council. The headline in bold on the pages of *Noddwr Llyfrau Cymraeg* (the magazine of the book societies) was 'Union dies – Council born!'[9]

The new body had deep roots in the voluntary sector, an ethos which persisted for many years. Efforts to persuade central government to fund it failed (regrettably, as will be seen below), but the sum of £28,000 was obtained from local authorities, so affirming the close ties with Welsh local government which have continued to this day.[10] In the range and size of its membership the governing body was of its time, including representatives of the local authorities along with the county chief librarians and representatives of the major bodies in education and culture. Nevertheless, it is significant that the first chairman selected was an academic (although the Constitution protected the interests of local government by insisting that the chair or vice-chair should be a representative of local government). Dr Henry Lewis, Professor of Welsh at the University College of Swansea, was appointed to the post – another powerful and influential figure who played a key role in the early years.

Though the government did not see fit to grant money to support the running costs of the new body, there had been a change of attitude in respect of support for Welsh-language publishing. In 1956 the Home Secretary, Henry Brooke, announced that a sum of £1,000 per annum had been earmarked 'to subsidise the production of new works in Welsh'.[11] This grant, though small, set an important precedent; it grew to £3,000 in 1960 with a promise of a yearly increase of £500 until a ceiling of £5,000 was reached. As this happened before the Books Council came into being, the task of administering 'the government grant' was entrusted to the Board of the University of Wales Press. Two decades later, the Welsh Office decided to transfer responsibility to the Books Council, but not without fundamental changes in the means of distributing the grant, as will be seen below.

The Books Council itself developed step by step. Almost five years went by before the first full-time organiser was appointed; until then it was Alun Edwards himself, with the aid of his staff at the library, and in particular Enid Roberts (later the Canon Enid Morgan), who did the work. But the search continued for a suitable full-time organiser and after long enquiry two names came to the fore: Dafydd Orwig and Alun Creunant Davies.[12] I heard Dafydd Orwig say on more than one occasion that he was more than happy to give way to Alun Creunant.

Alun Creunant was at the time headmaster of Llangeitho primary school in Ceredigion, and had come to the attention of Alun Edwards and others as an energetic young man who was active not only in his locality but also at a national level as the secretary of Undeb Cenedlaethol Athrawon Cymru (UCAC), the Welsh teachers' union. His administrative skills were therefore acknowledged, as were his gifts as a compère of eisteddfodau and a lay preacher. But although Alun Edwards and Alun Creunant had much in common, they were, deep down, very different in character. According to R. Gerallt Jones:

> Just as the fire and energy, single-mindedness and even occasionally blinkered attitude of Alun R. Edwards had been essential to start the enterprise, and to nudge it forward step by step, the equanimity and practical common sense of the new organiser were just what was needed in the budding organisation which was to grow eventually into a national institution of primary importance, complex and varied in its nature and structure.[13]

Alun Creunant stayed at the helm for twenty-two years (1965–87) and under his leadership the Books Council grew into a significant national body. To all intents and purposes the organisation in 1965 was a one-man band, but by the time of his retirement in 1987 the Council had a staff of 26 and a turnover of some half a million pounds. It also possessed two buildings – the headquarters, Castell Brychan, a splendid building overlooking Cardigan Bay, and a purpose-built distribution centre designed to support distribution and wholesale activities.

It is fair to say that the first priority in the early days was to support public libraries, and Alun Edwards strongly influenced the work programme. Librarians were begging for more popular material for readers of Welsh, especially fiction, and the Books Council was expected to make plans immediately to improve the situation. The other priority was to develop schemes to promote reading and ensure books were publicised as widely as possible.

The author grant was devised as a small remuneration for authors of popular material (the original sum was £3 per thousand words), and by a co-operative agreement between libraries, the books supported were given a guaranteed sale of 300–500 copies, purchased centrally for libraries. A Publications Panel was established to administer the scheme, and over a number of years the panel performed a valuable service in acknowledging the work of authors and supporting publishers by means of direct purchase. Rather than flood the market with popular novels, a series of books for libraries only was established. Islwyn Ffowc Elis was appointed to lead these programmes, and through his efforts and those of his successor, Vic John, dozens of books were published, including a number of translations of foreign novels.

On the promotional side *Llais Llyfrau* supplanted the *Noddwr* and became an essential tool for publicity for Welsh books (and later for books in English) for a period of thirty-five years, from 1964 to 1999. Numerous promotional schemes were also developed: among the most important were book quizzes for school pupils, book festivals and book campaigns. A book campaign had been run by Urdd Gobaith Cymru since the mid-1930s and was a useful way of selling books through the agency of school pupils who distributed catalogues door to door and collected orders.[14] Every one of these schemes proved successful and the quizzes and competitions for children are still flourishing.

From the early days, however, Alun Creunant was sensitive to the needs of the publishing industry, and establishing a book distribution service for publishers and booksellers was a priority.[15] This was a far-reaching step and he could hardly have foreseen the huge developments at the centre in recent years. It was also an early sign of the importance Alun Creunant attached to direct support for the publishing industry.

Two developments stand out during Alun Creunant's time as director. One is the growth of core services. Within two years of his taking over, the Welsh Arts Council had come into being as a branch of the British body. A number of imaginative directors were appointed to be responsible for different branches of the arts, among them Meic Stephens, a native of Pontypridd who had mastered Welsh as an adult and who embraced not only the Welsh language but also the two literatures of Wales. It was his vision, with Alun Creunant's approval, to establish central services in order to raise the standard of book production and publishing in Wales, and during the 1970s a number of specialist departments were created at the Books Council to offer services to publishers: editing, design, publicity and marketing (though not established in that order).[16]

Such services were badly needed. Wales's publishers were, on the whole, printer-publishers, and in those days, expertise on the publishing side was scarce. There was certainly no tradition of professional editors and designers. If any editing was done, it was by local teachers or ministers, and local art teachers and artists were often ready to use their skills in designing dustjackets.

This determined effort to raise standards had far-reaching consequences; it was also the beginning of a change in the Council's function from a body concentrating on the supply of popular books to meet the needs of public libraries to a body offering professional services to the publishing industry in Wales. More important still, the Welsh Arts Council was willing to fund these developments. Thus the Books Council now had two sources of funding: the local authorities and the Welsh Arts Council. And in the long run, Arts Council funding was a much greater share.

That was not without its problems. The Welsh Arts Council, even in these early days, took an interventionist approach, and wanted to see the Books Council turning its attention more to the promotion of literary material at the expense of the popular. This was understandable, given that the proper business of the Arts Council's Literature Committee was to support the creative artist and promote the writing and publication of literary works of a high standard. The emphasis of the Books Council was, however, different in that it concentrated on the needs of readers above all, with the long-term aim of nurturing a new generation of readers of Welsh. This required the availability of a variety of interesting and readable texts for different kinds of readers, and as popular books were scarce, improving provision in that sphere had to be a priority. The result was conflict between two mind sets – one represented by Meic Stephens and the other by Alun Edwards. It took all Alun Creunant's diplomatic skills to steer a middle course between the two!

To give one example: Alun Edwards enjoyed giving the impression that he had little truck with poetry. He was often heard to say that Wales had produced enough poetry 'to free-wheel to the end of the century'! On the other hand, the literature director of the Welsh Arts Council was dismissive of the need for a supply of light romantic novels in the Mills & Boon mould. To him this was a worthless initiative, and nothing raised his hackles so much as hearing Alun Edwards speaking passionately about the need for one hundred novels, fifteen biographies, and thirteen travel books every year. This appeal was one he made often.[17]

The second key development during Alun Creunant's time was the taking of responsibility for distributing grants to publishers. In 1979, following the publication of a report by the Council for the Welsh Language (a consultative body established to advise the Secretary of State),[18] the government announced a brand new grant of £55,000 to support leisure reading for children and magazines for children and adults, and the Books Council was invited to administer the grant.[19] This was a very important development, because until then the only support for children's books was the scheme operated by the Welsh Joint Education Committee (WJEC), which catered for the needs of schools. The government grant referred to above, which was administered by the Board of the University of Wales Press, was restricted to books for adults. Two years later, procedures were further rationalised when the government grant for books for adults was also transferred to the Books Council.[20] (The sum total available for distribution in 1981–82 was £285,000.) This was another milestone development in the history of the Council. As well as offering services to the publishing industry, the Books Council was now responsible for distributing grants to publishers across a broad spectrum. The WJEC continued to administer a publishing scheme for schools, and the Arts Council continued to provide grants for literary books and magazines. The remit of the Books Council, therefore, was general books for children and adults and leisure magazines for children and adults. No doubt there was a widespread view that the Books Council would concentrate on material of popular appeal, but a conscious decision was taken to interpret the term 'general books' in a broad sense, and to support a range of books that were good of their kind, including some literary works and critical studies. This was a clear sign that the Books Council now considered itself a body which served the totality of Welsh publishing. And in the wake of the new funding available for leisure reading for children, there was an opportunity to make every effort to provide a wealth of material by responding to requests from publishers and by direct commissioning by the Books Council itself. So began a period in which provision for children and young people was transformed.

John Morris (later Lord Morris of Aberavon) was the Secretary of State at the Welsh Office who gave these new responsibilities to the Books Council.[21] He proved a great benefactor to the books industry, and although the time was ripe for change, it was certainly a great help that the Secretary of State had links with the world of publishing. His father-in-law was none other than Edward Lewis of Gwasg Gomer, one of the sons of J. D. Lewis of Llandysul, and grandfather of the present owner.

Not that publishers welcomed the change with open arms. It was one thing to have a new grant for children's books, but moving the adult grant from the University Press to the Books Council denoted a fundamental change in the way the grants were administered. The University Press had performed the service for nothing over the years – more or less as a favour – and had adopted the simplest method possible to administer the grant. Money would be divided out between the applications submitted, without requiring any more information than the book's title and a broad estimate of its length. Even those details would scarcely be known, since most books were not complete at the time a grant was offered towards publishing costs. It was emphasised that the Books Council was expected to operate much more strictly: assessing and selecting completed texts, and rejecting typescripts that did not deserve public funding. And the Council was expected to appoint a panel of experts to make these decisions.

It could be said that Alun Edwards was quite right when he warned the Books Council of the dangers of administering grants. He knew well enough that such was not the way to win friends. Indeed, the storm broke before work had even begun. The pages of *Barn* and *Y Faner* at the beginning of the 1980s reveal the strength of feeling among some of the publishers about the change.

'Censorship', 'Uniformity', 'Nationalising the Publishing Industry' – these were some of the headlines in the Welsh-language press at the time.[22] But only a small few were intent on wrecking the structure before work began: the majority accepted that any increase in support from the public purse would inevitably lead to a greater level of accountability. And Alun Creunant succeeded in gaining the co-operation of most, although one or two challenged him all the way.

One advantage which accrued from administering the government grant was that the Books Council began to deal directly with civil servants and government ministers. This led to project funding becoming available for a number of activities, particularly in the field of children's books. Clwb Sbondonics and its lively magazine were established in 1983 in a bid to attract children to books and encourage them to buy them. The club was organised through primary schools and proved an excellent vehicle for introducing books to children and their parents, thus promoting the habit of reading at home. A grant was also made for the purchase of a colourful exhibition van to travel around schools in Wales and showcase publications. A decade later, in 1992, a team of officers was appointed to introduce and sell educational material to primary and secondary schools in close co-operation with bookshops. This grew into an essential marketing service for all Welsh schools and a service much appreciated by the education sector and the publishing industry, and also by those organisations which support the publication of educational materials.

The Welsh Arts Council also took an interest in the field of children's books at this time. Thanks to the efforts of people like Mairwen Gwynn Jones and Geraint Lewis, a Children's Literature Panel was established as a sub-committee of the main Literature Committee, and both of them in turn chaired the panel. One of the most ambitious of the panel's schemes in its early years was the establishment of a children's literature centre with an international dimension at the College of Librarianship Wales in 1979. Menna Lloyd Williams was appointed head.

For a number of reasons, the centre did not develop in accordance with the original vision, particularly on the international side, and the College of Librarianship lost interest in it. As a result, it was moved to the Books Council's new headquarters at Castell Brychan in 1981, and the two institutions co-operated successfully for a decade. In 1990, at the request of the Arts Council and the centre itself, it was incorporated into the Books Council and a new Children's Books Department was established under the leadership of Menna Lloyd Williams. This became a key department as the Council put greater emphasis on schemes to encourage children and young people to read, and provide suitable material for them.

When Alun Creunant decided to retire in 1987 I was privileged to succeed him and served as director for twenty-two years (1987–2009). I had served my apprenticeship at the Arts Council before moving to the Books Council in November 1976, and had been at the centre of the exciting plans to provide specialist central services to publishers. I was also eager to see the Books Council become an acknowledged development body for the whole industry, both Welsh and English medium. This, for me, was the logical next step. There had been some movement in that direction already in those aspects of the work supported by the Arts Council: the Welsh name of the organisation was changed in 1995 from Cyngor Llyfrau Cymraeg (referring to Welsh-language books) to Cyngor Llyfrau Cymru (referring to books from Wales in both languages). I was also convinced that the key to attracting further funding to develop the publishing industry was showing excellence in all aspects of the work. What was needed was a wide variety of publications of the highest standard for all sorts of readers and all ranges of ability – from the youngest children to the oldest readers – and a systematic approach to filling gaps in provision. Above all, I believed that a greater demand for books must be created and sales increased, and it was evident that the Distribution Centre had a key role to play, alongside the efforts of the publishers to market their own output.

The following twenty years witnessed a number of important developments. Possibly the most significant was the simplification of the funding structure and the placing of the Books Council on a surer financial footing. This was important, not only for ease of administration, but also because it paved the way for all sorts of important and necessary developments and provided the opportunity to attract substantial additional funding for the development of the industry. But change was not plain sailing, as will be seen.

One advantage of the way in which the Books Council was established in the early 1960s was the untrammelled freedom it enjoyed to do its work. Very few conditions were attached to the grant funding, and there were no complex accounting procedures involved. Yet this had its disadvantages. By the end of the 1980s and the beginning of the 1990s the Books Council's financial position was rather insecure: it was dependent on contributions from individual local authorities (who were either very supportive or lukewarm or worse), and from the Literature Committee of the Arts Council. By then the latter was viewing support for the specialist departments as a burden that tied up money which could be used to start new initiatives. This was a particularly frustrating period for the Arts Council's Literature Committee, as the literature budget was under pressure, and the assiduous efforts of the committee to secure a bigger slice of the arts cake had failed.[23] That in turn sharpened the focus on the Books Council, far and away its largest client, and there was certainly a feeling that the mission of the Books Council was increasingly marginal to a committee which existed primarily to support literary works and the creative artist. The natural place to turn to was the Welsh Office; the Books Council already had a foot in the door, as it was the Welsh Office which provided the grants it administered. And it was no bad thing that the Arts Council – albeit for different reasons – was also keen to see the Welsh Office funding the Books Council.

So began the struggle to persuade central government to take financial responsibility for the Books Council, a struggle which saw many futile steps along the way. It took six years for the Welsh Office to assume responsibility for the Arts Council's share of the core funding. That came about through a complex arrangement whereby one body reduced its contribution while the other increased it step by step. By 1996 this process was complete, leaving only two elements to the Books Council's core funding, namely the local authorities (eight of them, each contributing individually) and the Welsh Office.

But at the very time when arrangements were being simplified, the reorganisation of local government in 1996 complicated matters again. From then on twenty-two (rather than eight) authorities had to be approached individually for sums which in themselves were quite small but which in total represented an important part of the organisation's core funding. The chairman of the Books Council at the time was Dafydd Orwig, and as a local government leader he worked hard during the year before reorganisation to get an agreement between authorities on a formula for remitting the money. That was as much as could be achieved under the circumstances, and he himself knew as well as anybody that the formula had no statutory force and would not survive difficult times.

Then, to complicate matters further, the Welsh Language Board came into being as a statutory body in 1993. As a result, all Welsh Office grants for promoting the Welsh language – grants which had developed during the time of Wyn Roberts (later Lord Roberts of Conwy) as a Welsh Office minister – were transferred to the Board. These grants were by now substantial, as Wyn Roberts had shown considerable support for Welsh-language culture over the years. The transfer was achieved in two stages: half a million to begin with, made up of sums which supported a range of bodies in the voluntary sector, from the Welsh Young Farmers to Merched y Wawr, CYD (the Welsh Learners Association), Cyngor Ysgolion Sul (the Sunday Schools Council), and others. In 1996 the intention was to transfer the budget for the four remaining bodies, namely the National Eisteddfod, the Urdd, Mudiad Ysgolion Meithrin (the Nursery Schools Movement), and the Books Council. Several of the bodies involved appealed strongly against this decision, and perhaps the deciding factor in the case of the Books Council was its involvement with English-language as well as Welsh-language publishing: as a result, it would not be appropriate for it to come under the aegis of a Board that dealt solely with the interests of the Welsh language. In the end a compromise was reached. The Welsh Office would continue to be responsible for the core funding or day to day running costs of the Books Council, but the publishing grants budget, which related to the Welsh language alone, would now be channelled through the Language Board. The Council would therefore be obliged to make an annual application to the Language Board for a sum of money for publishing, and would be accountable to the Board for its expenditure.

It was an unsatisfactory settlement to say the least, but the compromise proved crucial when it came to reversing the decision six years later, in the early days of the Welsh Assembly Government. In 2002 the funding link with local authorities and the Language Board was severed, and the Books Council became wholly accountable to the Welsh Assembly Government. It had taken forty-one years to change the funding basis, forty-one years of piecemeal funding which in the end proved unsustainable. There is no doubt that this was a major victory, perhaps the greatest in the history of the Books Council, for the succeeding decade was a time of considerable expansion and development, as the Assembly Government recognised the importance of investing in the publishing industry. Shortly afterwards, in April 2003, with the approval of the Assembly Government, the Arts Council transferred all its publishing responsibilities (for literary publishing in both languages) to the Books Council, so allowing the Council the opportunity at last to develop the industry as a whole.

One of the changes which occurred in the wake of the new accountability was the shift of emphasis from central services to developing specialist skills in the publishing houses themselves. The Books Council's view was that some things were better and more efficiently serviced centrally, to the benefit of every sector of the trade (for instance distribution, the task of supplying orders to bookshops on behalf of publishers; also the development of sophisticated electronic information systems such as the Gwales website), but that other aspects would be far better dealt with by the publishers themselves – the commissioning of books, creative editing in co-operation with the author, the marketing of particular titles and so on. Such devolution had financial implications. In the early days of the Assembly Government there were good opportunities to secure additional funding if strong arguments, based on sound evidence, could be put forward on behalf of the industry. During the time of Jenny Randerson as Culture Minister, for instance, a task and finish group was established in 2001, chaired by her deputy, Delyth Evans, to make a full study of the whole field, and at the end of a detailed process the minister was persuaded that the field of Welsh-language publishing was greatly in need of further investment.

This was a step change. The best efforts had not succeeded in obtaining any increase during the six years in which the Language Board had been responsible for administering the budget for publishing. Those were arid and depressing years. But thanks to Jenny Randerson, and in particular to the fair and thorough work of Delyth Evans, a new opportunity arose in 2002 when the Assembly Government decided that the publishing grants should be increased by eighty per cent over three years. This gave the main publishers the chance to start developing balanced publishing programmes and to adopt a policy of commissioning books from authors.

Direct commissioning by the Books Council thus came to an end, to all intents and purposes. The Children's Books Commissioning Panel, in particular, had been in existence since the early days of administering the grants, and had done admirable work for two decades in recognising and filling gaps in provision, devising fiction series for all age ranges and dozens of individual titles with a high standard of content and design. But it was time to put faith in the publishers and as there was a new body, ACCAC, the Qualifications, Curriculum and Assessment Authority for Wales, which was commissioning a wide range of materials for schools, there was an opportunity to begin concentrating more on books for adults.

It was made clear to the Books Council that the industry was expected to deliver on its commitments, as everyone accepted. We were accountable to the Assembly Government for the funding, and fully understood that hard facts were needed as proof of success and value for money. Considerable pressure was placed on the publishers in this period, and more on the Books Council itself, not only to justify the investment but also to prepare the way for further growth in the future.

It was all worth the effort, and no-one was prouder than the publishers themselves when in 2009 the Heritage Minister, Alun Ffred Jones, was persuaded, just as severe restrictions were being placed on the expenditure of public money, to invest an additional £300,000 per annum in the Welsh publishing industry. Every part of the industry had come together about a year before to present a case – publishers, booksellers, the Writers' Union and the Books Council, and a united front was presented along with evidence of success.

A substantial portion of the additional money received between 2002 and 2005 was allocated towards improving authors' fees. As the Writers' Union had foreseen, this was to bring huge dividends, and within a comparatively short time, literary critics like Professor John Rowlands were speaking of a 'mini-renaissance' in Welsh-language-fiction.[24] Dr Simon Brooks said:

> One of the obvious things is that Welsh literature is experiencing a kind of golden age . . . Every year there is a crop of novels, short stories, biographies appearing which are excellent, of the highest possible standard.[25]

Reading groups experienced growth and positive press attention was reflected in sales figures. Thus when the further increase in the grant came from 2009 onward, emphasis was placed on appointing creative editors in the main publishing houses, to work hand in hand with authors, especially new authors, to improve the content of texts. The minister was also persuaded that more resources were needed for book design and illustration.

Publishers deserve full credit for their key role in this revival. They are small in number, but they are more alert than ever to the demands of the audience in both Welsh and English, and they make every effort to nurture authors. But it is the additional resources which have made a real difference, and there is no doubt that the situation today would not be so encouraging had not the Books Council come directly under the aegis of the Assembly Government in 2002. That gave the officers of the Books Council the opportunity to put their case directly to ministers in close co-operation with the industry and the Writers' Union. Librarians also gave every assistance and support.

The publishing industry is a mixed economy and the relationship between the private and public sectors is at best one of creative tension. Perhaps it is even more difficult for a body like the Books Council, which for years offered practical assistance to publishers but which developed into a body which also awarded grants to them – with all the demands associated with such a responsibility – while still offering services.

This tension, which is unavoidable, may be creative, but can become destructive when one side doubts the integrity of the other, with consequent reproaches and arguments, sometimes in public. On the whole the publishing industry has succeeded in avoiding this by settling differences within the industry itself. It would be misleading to give the impression that it has always been easy, especially at a time of rapid change when major improvements were needed. Both sides were required to show maturity, but there is no doubt that it was this, and the united front shown in presenting arguments and priorities, that was the key to attracting additional resources.

The total budget for publishing grants in 2002 was £623,000 (a sum which had seen no increase in six years). It had been increased to £1.6 million in 2011, not including a sum for the online news service, *Golwg 360*, or the grants now available for English-language publishing. If those be added in, the total was £2.7 million, a far cry from the £1,000 announced by Henry Brooke over half a century ago.

When the Books Council assumed responsibility for distributing grants for English-language publications in 2003, the Arts Council insisted on an assurance that there would be no diminution of support for literary titles, either for books or periodicals. The Books Council fully accepted that literary provision must be safeguarded, but at the same time it was made clear that the long-term aim would be to seek to ensure a wider range of English-language books from Welsh publishers, along with a strategy to broaden the market for what was produced. It was accepted that additional resources would be needed to do so; the fact that the Council already had considerable experience of administering grants was a help, and additional staff were also appointed, individuals with specific qualifications in the field of Welsh writing in English, to lead the development under the guidance of an enthusiastic and committed panel.

Professor M. Wynn Thomas, as Professor of English and director of CREW (Centre for Research into the English Literature and Language of Wales) at Swansea University, had been urging the Assembly Government since its inception to take an interest in English writing in Wales. It was a fortunate coincidence that the Assembly's Committee for Culture, the Welsh Language and Sport, chaired by Rosemary Butler, chose to concentrate on this area for a whole term shortly after the Books Council was given the responsibility for administering grants for English-language publications. A number of individuals were invited to give evidence to the committee, and an open invitation was issued to anyone with an interest in the field to make written submissions.

Much work went on in the background to ensure that the review was as comprehensive as possible, with clear and practical recommendations to encourage development. The final report, *English Medium Writing in Wales*, which was published in 2004, was warmly welcomed and unanimously approved by all political parties.[26] As a result, the minister, Alun Pugh, offered the Books Council the sum of £250,000 to begin work on implementing the recommendations. This was a small amount in the context of the report, which contained ambitious and far-reaching recommendations, but it was a start, and the money was gratefully received. The minister's own priority was to establish a new series of books bearing the title 'Library of Wales' – a series of new editions of books which had been out of print for years and which were considered part of the literary heritage of everyone interested in English literature from Wales. It was Professor Wynn Thomas who submitted the idea to the committee, on the basis of his experience of the series 'Library of America', and it caught the imagination of committee members and the minister. This would hardly transform English-language publishing in Wales, but civil servants were helpful in ensuring that part of the funding could be used to begin supporting books which had potential to reach a wider audience, and to invest in marketing programmes to promote them. The aim was to encourage publishers to create an additional income stream which would help to support more specialised books and strengthen the publishing houses, eventually making them less dependent on public funding. As the development of publishing in English is the subject of another chapter, there is no need to elaborate here, other than to emphasise the commitment of the Books Council to the two literatures of Wales and its desire to do more as resources would allow.

In discussing these many developments, it is important not to forget the value of the core services which are essential to the organisation's mission – editing, design, marketing and distribution. The contribution of the editorial and design departments of the Books Council to the raising of standards through the years cannot be overstated, and though some of the main publishers now have their own specialist staff, the two small departments continue to provide an indispensable service to the industry and give advice and support as required.

By far the largest division of the Books Council is the Distribution Centre, which has grown and adapted over the years as customer demands have changed and expectations have risen. The service was established as a business venture from the start and the Centre has never received any subvention from the public purse towards its running costs. Its function was simply to supply orders to bookshops on behalf of Welsh publishers, and a centralised scheme was of enormous benefit to publishers and booksellers alike. Bookshops could order all titles from Welsh publishing houses from one place and deal with one supplier; publishers could leave a supply of every title at the Distribution Centre in the knowledge that they would receive prompt payment for every copy sold. The operation began on a very small scale with three members of staff working from rooms not far from Aberystwyth railway station, and an annual turnover of £16,000 (net) in 1966–67, which in three years rose to £60,000. Within a few years the service had moved from Alexandra Road to premises in Gray's Inn Road, which had the luxury of a lift to move books from one floor to the next. That celebrated machine was allegedly an agricultural relic! Bus services were used in the early days to transport books to shops, but as the workload increased, vans were acquired which visited the main shops once a week (an arrangement made possible by the fact that the vans also carried books for the interlending service between libraries). Representatives were also appointed to collect orders from shops.

In 1977 the Centre moved to two factory units on the new Glanyrafon industrial estate in Llanbadarn Fawr, which had been built by the Development Board for Rural Wales. Facilities here were of course considerably better, and when it was evident that more space was needed the Development Board offered to erect a new building designed to the Centre's specification. The present building was occupied in 1981, at about the same time as the main office moved from Queen's Square to Castell Brychan; the accommodation was rented to begin with, but advantage was taken in a few years of the opportunity to purchase the building. When I became director in 1987 the workload had increased enormously, but the use of technology was still limited, and though the Council had invested in a computer in 1981 (the Burroughs B92), there were no appropriate management or stock control systems. From the beginning of the 1990s onward great emphasis was placed on automation, experimenting initially with a fairly simple system designed specifically for our needs by CPL from north Wales. In 1996, with substantial support from various public sources (including the National Lottery, European funding and the Welsh Office), the Centre invested in systems produced by Vista Computer Services, as they were then called. Vista specialised in systems for the book distribution industry and their systems were in use at the leading distribution and wholesale centres in Britain. This was a far-reaching development, as the company was constantly improving the software, which led in the end to the Gwales developments (from 1999 on) which are the subject of another chapter.

Over the years a number of reports were commissioned from specialists in the field with the aim of improving and developing the distribution service, and changes have been implemented regularly. Some of these were controversial, such as changing to a pattern of daily distribution by professional couriers, introducing formal contracts between the Centre and its customers, and adopting stricter controls over cash flow and debts. It was all necessary for a business which by 2010 had an annual turnover of £3.3 million net, and close on £5 million gross. And it is fair to say that the Centre evokes admiration in a number of countries which, like Wales, have minority-language publishing.

Central services have seen an increased emphasis over the years on promotional schemes which led directly to sales. Even in the Children's Books Department the magazine *Sgwarnog* had to give way to *Sbondonics*, and subsequently to sales leaflets. But the organisation continued to be enthusiastic for the promotion of reading, and the tradition of regular co-operation with libraries and schools on particular schemes continued. Two opportunities arose to co-ordinate a National Year of Reading (in 1998–99 and in 2008), and there was enthusiastic co-operation with a range of new partners in the private and voluntary sectors as well as the public sector. There was a substantial difference between the two campaigns. By the time of the second campaign, there was an emphasis on promoting reading through all kinds of media, without exclusive concentration on traditional print. Technology has impinged on all aspects of the Books Council's work and by now electronic publishing is affirming itself alongside the traditional.

The last half century has seen huge developments, and there has been a readiness to embrace change and to take advantage of new opportunities. A small, fragile organisation has grown into a public body of importance, directly sponsored by the Welsh Government, and its methods of work have been transformed in accordance with the demands of a new age. Throughout the period the Books Council has been very fortunate in its chairmen and honorary officers – gifted individuals who gave generously of their time and expertise without remuneration – and the organisation is much indebted to them all. In the same way, the salaried staff have given untiring service to the institution and it was good to be able to bring together present and former members as part of the fiftieth anniversary celebrations. Although the Books Council of today is not the same as the 'mustard seed' planted at the beginning of the 1960s, there is no doubt that the values associated with the early pioneers continue to inspire the latest generation of leaders – commitment, a missionary spirit, a willingness to be bold, and above all a passionate love of language and culture.

Gwerfyl Pierce Jones joined the staff of the Books Council in 1976. She was Director of the Council from 1987 until her retirement in 2009.

Notes

[1] Gwilym Huws, 'Welsh-language publishing 1919 to 1995', in Philip Henry Jones and Eiluned Rees (eds), *A Nation and its Books. A History of the Book in Wales* (Aberystwyth, National Library of Wales in association with Aberystwyth Centre for the Book, 1998), pp. 341–3.

[2] Home Office, *Report of the Committee on Welsh Language Publishing / Adroddiad y Pwyllgor Cyhoeddi Llyfrau Cymraeg* (London, HMSO, 1952).

[3] Ibid., p. 5.

[4] Emlyn Evans, 'Cofio Dafydd', in Ieuan Wyn (ed.), *Cofio Dafydd Orwig* (Caernarfon, Gwasg Gwynedd, 1977), pp. 14–16; Emlyn Evans, *O'r Niwl a'r Anialwch: Cynnyrch Chwarter Canrif* (Dinbych, Gwasg Gee, 1991), pp. 214–18.

[5] Evans, 'Cofio Dafydd', p. 16.

[6] Evans, *O'r Niwl a'r Anialwch*, pp. 218–21.

[7] Alun R. Edwards, *Yr Hedyn Mwstard: Atgofion Alun R. Edwards* (Llandysul, Gwasg Gomer, 1980), pp. 78–85. It is to this volume that the title of this chapter refers.

[8] Ibid., p. 49.

[9] *Noddwr Llyfrau Cymraeg*, 7 (1961), 1–3.

[10] Edwards, *Yr Hedyn Mwstard*, p. 94.

[11] Council for Wales and Monmouthshire, *Report on the Welsh Language Today* (London, HMSO, 1963).

[12] See the article on Alun Creunant Davies in *Dictionary of Welsh Biography online* (http://wbo.llgc.org.uk/).

[13] R. Gerallt Jones, 'Alun R. Edwards a'i Gyngor', in Rheinallt Llwyd (ed.), *Gwarchod y Gwreiddiau* (Llandysul, Gwasg Gomer, 1996), p. 70.

[14] R.E. Griffith, *Urdd Gobaith Cymru. Cyfrol I: 1922–1945* (Aberystwyth, Cwmni Urdd Gobaith Cymru, 1971), pp. 204–5.

[15] Cyngor Llyfrau Cymraeg, *Annual Report 1966–67*, p. 6.

[16] Meic Stephens, *Hunangofiant Meic Stephens: Cofnodion* (Tal-y-bont, Y Lolfa, 2012), p. 92.

[17] Edwards, *Yr Hedyn Mwstard*, p. 88.

[18] Cyngor yr Iaith Gymraeg, *Cyhoeddi yn yr Iaith Gymraeg / Publishing in the Welsh Language* (Cardif, HMSO, 1978).

[19] Cyngor Llyfrau Cymraeg, *Annual Report 1978–79*, pp. 13–16.

[20] Cyngor Llyfrau Cymraeg, *Annual Report 1980–81*, p. 9.

[21] Lord Morris of Aberavon, *Fifty Years in Politics and the Law* (Cardiff, University of Wales Press, 2011), pp. 155–7.

[22] See for instance *Barn*, 220 (Mai 1981) and *Y Faner*, 19 June 1981.

[23] Stephens, *Hunangofiant*, pp. 116–20.

[24] Personal correspondence.

[25] Quoted in *Golwg*, 21 April 2011, 8.

[26] National Assembly for Wales, Culture, Welsh Language and Sport Committee, *English Medium Writing in Wales* (Cardiff, National Assembly for Wales, 2004).

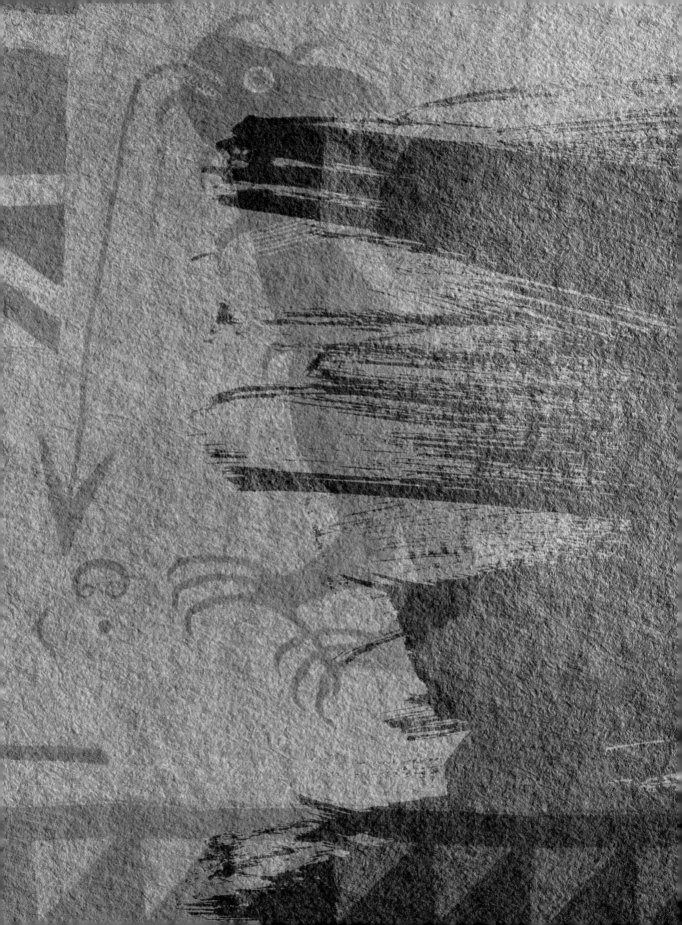

Cloudbusting

*How Welsh-language publishers and
publishers in Wales worked together to respond
to financial cuts during a period of recession*

Cloudbusting

Elwyn Jones discusses how Welsh-language publishers and publishers in Wales worked together to respond to financial cuts during a period of recession

During July 2012, a number of the Books Council's former and current employees came together in Aberystwyth to celebrate the Council's fiftieth anniversary. It was of course a happy occasion and due tribute was paid to the achievements over the years. Some remembered the early days, others were part of exciting developments in regard to services to the publishing industry, and others again reminisced about distributing books via the bus routes of Wales!

But the event was overshadowed by dark clouds also, as the institution was very aware of the financial cuts that it faced during a period of general recession. The fears were sadly realised and the Council did face years of financial cuts.

A real crisis arrived in 2016, when the Welsh Government threatened a cut of ten per cent in the Council's funding, an action which would have undermined the previous period's developments and endangered the future of the industry. Fortunately, there was fierce opposition to the proposed cut from various parts of the publishing sector, including both publishers and booksellers, but above all the writers, who organised a successful petition. Undoubtedly, one of the key strengths of the campaign was the cooperation between the Welsh- and English-language halves of the publishing world and there was great relief when the decision was eventually overturned.

The serious nature of the recession was reflected in the reduction in book sales through the Council's Distribution Centre, with the public, libraries and the education sector all facing austerity and cut-backs in expenditure. A number of booksellers noted that this was the most difficult period they had ever faced.

However, even in a period of austerity, the Council maintained its belief in the need to continue with developments in the industry. Thus it was, that even in these challenging times, plans were put in place to support and strengthen the publishing companies. A programme of training and mentoring was organised in the varied aspects of business and financial management, copyright regulations and exports. Investment had already been made to support creative editors and marketing officers at the publishing houses, and this aspect was further developed by holding courses and discussion forums for booksellers and librarians.

The flip side of this was to encourage the individual publishers to ensure balance in their publishing schedule – between good sellers and other volumes of a more literary nature – in order to meet specific sales targets. Naturally, such changes to the usual way of doing things was not easy or welcomed by everyone, but the Council felt this was the only way to ensure a thriving and successful publishing industry.

The book trade was not the only thing to come under the microscope; a detailed review was undertaken of the Welsh and English-language magazines during the same period, leading to a new franchise arrangement and challenging them also to reach more readers in both print and digital formats.

Perhaps 'digital' has become a little too fashionable a word for some people, including government ministers, with many foretelling the end of the print book in favour of electronic copies. This has not been the case, and the publishers responded positively by publishing ebooks, while realising that print versions still drove the business model. An important principle established at this time was to ensure that bookshops benefitted from the new technology by receiving commission on any sale, whether print or digital, made through the Gwales website.

As regards Welsh-language books, it was reassuring that regular surveys by Beaufort Research found an appetite for reading, with the percentage of those reading at least one book a year rising from 26% to 43% between 2003 and 2012. It was also a time when English-language authors from Wales received increasing attention in the British press.

Following the decision of the Welsh Government to review the work of its sponsored bodies, the Rolph report was commissioned on the work of the Council, which confirmed its essential role at the heart of the industry in Wales. The report was also helpful in reforming the Council's financial organisation, and by the time the Medwin Hughes report appeared some years later, it was able to confirm that further steps had been taken to develop the industry.

One of the areas that developed most during this time was that of books for children. Fortunately, additional finance was secured from the Welsh Government to commission a series of English-language books which reflected the background and interests of young readers. As part of this investment programme, a brand new publishing company, Firefly, was supported, and to date it has made a significant contribution to this field.

Attention was also given to the field of Welsh-language books for children, by commissioning a report from Mairwen Prys Jones, who had years of experience in this area. This lead, in turn, to the Rosser report (see Siwan Rosser's essay below) which paid particular attention to adaptations, and led to further investment in original books for children and young people (and in time to innovative, varied series such as that described by Elgan Rhys, below).

Fortunately, the Government's Education Department saw the importance of securing a good supply of Welsh-language and bilingual books for all of the schools in Wales; a decision which was welcomed by both teachers and the publishing industry alike. Unfortunately, some difficult decisions had to be taken, such as winding up the children's book club which was delivered through schools. As the patterns of book buying had changed, and considering the increasing pressures on teachers, the model was no longer sustainable.

It should be acknowledged also that not every child or adult is a keen reader, and so particular effort was made through schemes such as Reading Communities to reach reluctant readers in deprived areas and to provide suitable material through the Stori Sydyn/Quick Reads series. Reading Communities was such a success that an invitation was received to make a presentation on the scheme as part of the educational strand of the Frankfurt Book Fair. These were the kind of schemes that Kay Andrews had in mind when she noted the importance of the book industry in her report on combating childhood poverty. One disappointment for the Council was the failure to gain a Lottery grant during this period to hold a Reading City pilot in Swansea; such a scheme had first been tried in Seattle and had transformed reading in that city.

Despite the dark clouds referred to at the beginning having had a real impact on the publishing industry, the way the sector responded to these challenges by continuing to provide a varied and appealing choice for readers was enormously heartening.

Elwyn Jones was the Director and Chief Executive of the Books Council of Wales between 2009 and 2017.

Two Rivers
from a Common Spring

*How the Council became, and remains,
pivotal to the service of a vibrant publishing
industry working within two linguistic landscapes*

Two Rivers
from a Common Spring

*M. Wynn Thomas on how the Council became, and remains,
pivotal to the service of a vibrant publishing industry
working within two linguistic landscapes*

1901 was a watershed year in Welsh history. For the first time since the emergence of an embryonic 'Wales' a millennium and a half earlier, the language spoken by the majority of the country's population was definitively revealed (by government census) to be English (50.1%). The language shift thus confirmed had been completed with remarkable rapidity: barely half a century had passed since the incursion in great numbers into the south-eastern valleys of an increasingly anglophone population that had steadily consolidated, in the interim, into an ostensibly 'alien' industrial proletariat. Culture shift, particularly as evidenced in an anglophone Welsh literature, was slower to follow. Writing in English had, of course, emanated from Wales since early in the modern era, but it had usually inclined towards the 'settler' in character, and had always been clearly peripheral to the Welsh-language cultural life of the country. During the last decades of the nineteenth century, anglophone novels that were more evidently, even sometimes committedly, Welsh in character had begun to proliferate, but it was not until the 1930s that an undisputed 'native' generation of conspicuous talent emerged, many members of which were intent on an authentic recording of the compelling past and present history of their remarkable 'valleys' society.

As Glyn Jones, one of the undoubted luminaries of this 'Dylan Thomas' generation shrewdly noted, the majority of these writers were themselves the products of 'language shift'. The offspring of Welsh-speaking parents, they had also been the products of the new anglophone (and in some ways anglicising) system of grammar schools. In the absence of any possibility of having their work published in a Wales bereft of publishers, they concentrated on a London market, and to some extent adjusted their writing to the tastes and expectations of an English readership. It would be another thirty years, at least, before Wales began to 'grow' a publishing industry of its own, and that as a result of a 'cultural revolution' during the sixties that was, in its way, the belated counterpart of, and corrective to, the culturally divisive industrial revolution that had brought a new, modern, anglophone Wales into being a century and more earlier.

Financially enabled and ideologically sponsored by British state initiatives, this cultural revolution involved a radical reconfiguration of the relations between anglophone and Welsh-speaking Wales that had largely obtained since around 1901. Those relations, mistrustful at best and hostile at worst, had come to be memorably symbolised by Caradoc Evans, whose singular collection of stories, *My People* (1915), had been welcomed by many of the 'Anglo-Welsh' generation of the thirties as a liberating exposé of the grotesque, morally malformed character of regressive, inbred Welsh-language culture. It took half a century, and crises in parallel (the contraction of Welsh-language society and the terminal decay of the anglophone society of industrial south Wales), to turn a settled mutual suspicion into a qualified mutual sympathy and a cautiously emergent sense of solidarity. As class identity on the one hand and linguistic identity on the other receded in this new post-industrial context, so a new shared sense of national identity began to emerge. These two separately threatened linguistic communities found themselves converging on a sense of a Wales at risk, partly defined by the inflammatory case of Tryweryn that highlighted the political impotence even of a pan-Wales will. Many young writers from both cultures, already sensitised by the 'événements' in Paris and the Civil Rights and anti-Vietnam movements in the USA, found themselves inclining towards engaged writing.

But even as Welsh writers, in both languages, began to embrace a 'counter-cultural' identity predicated in part on a radical critique of the established policies and practices of a conspicuously centralised, and anglocentric, British state, that state was proceeding to enact a generous programme of increasingly devolved public funding of the arts that was to enable Welsh writing in English (as in Welsh) to establish for the first time the rudiments of its own native support system.

The body established to implement this programme was the Arts Council – an agency that, like many of the prominent innovations of the Welfare State, was born of the beleaguered wartime British state's concern to foster a strong sense of collective identity. Two of its key initiators were Welsh: Sir William Emrys Williams and Dr. Thomas Jones. The government-funded Council for the Encouragement of Music and Drama was created in 1940 'to help promote and maintain British culture', and with the cessation of hostilities this mutated into an Arts Council of Great Britain with several 'regional' committees. Under the Royal Charter of 1967, the Welsh regional committee evolved into a Welsh Arts Council whose position, within what was the new federal structure of the Arts Council of Great Britain, guaranteed it a significant degree of autonomy. In its turn, the Welsh Arts Council established a number of lay committees to initiate and manage developments across all acknowledged major art forms, including literature (in both Welsh and English), and appointed specialist directors to serve and advise each of these committees.

The appointment of Meic Stephens as inaugural Director of Literature proved to be an inspired one, and led to a wholesale transformation, not only of the literary landscape, but of the entire book world in Wales. His visionary drive, combative nature and sense of cultural mission, informed as it was by a young practitioner's personal experience of the plight of a Welsh anglophone author, resulted, during the subsequent quarter century of his historic incumbency, not only in a range of measures to assist individual writers, but in the steady piecemeal construction, virtually from scratch, of the extensive infrastructure necessary for the creation and maintenance of a modern professional book industry. And at the very heart of the whole enterprise lay a convinced recognition that the glory of modern Wales lay in its bicultural character and a determination to ensure parity of respect and of treatment for both those cultures.

Through its enormously influential and powerful Literature Committee, the Welsh Arts Council not only provided authors with grants, it funded journals to publish and discuss their writing, 'grew' publishers to produce, market and distribute their work, encouraged radical improvements in design and quality of production, and even established a bookshop to showcase publications and assist sales. Complementing its support for a Welsh Academy, and (in due course) its foundation of a writers' centre, was an international programme to bring renowned writers like Ionesco, Margaret Atwood and Derek Walcott to Wales. It sent authors into schools, and through a series of pioneering publications – from anthologies to collections of reflective autobiographical essays by leadings writers; and from the remarkable Writers of Wales series to the momentous and monumental *Oxford Companion to the Literature of Wales* – it slowly but surely began to correct the shocking deficit (for which the secondary and HE systems of education deserved much of the blame) in modern Wales's awareness of its own literary past and present, an ignorance particularly evident with regard to its English-language writers. Awareness of the historic neglect of young readers led it to support a series of initiatives in the field of children's literature, including a new imprint specifically dedicated to producing English-language stories with Welsh themes and settings. By the time of Stephens' departure from the Welsh Arts Council in 1990, the literary landscape of Wales had been totally transformed, and not least that very extensive (and previously largely neglected) part of it that related to the country's anglophone authors.

Long before Stephens' departure, though, the writing was on the wall. He had come into post during the halcyon years of a Wilson government that, chivvied by Arts Council of Great Britain's chairman Arnold (Lord) Goodman and Arts Minister Jennie Lee, was relatively lavish in its support of culture, in the interests of honouring the old honourable Labour pledge to extend the privilege of enjoying high culture and of thus enriching sensibility from the wealthy upper classes to the population at large. But the advent of a crusadingly 'anti-paternalistic' Thatcher government heralded the dawn of a new individualistic age when the operations of culture, like those of virtually all others spheres of social activity, were to be regulated by market forces supposedly guaranteed to ensure the enhancement of personal freedoms. In 1982, Sir William Rees-Mogg was appointed Chair of the Arts Council with the specific brief of reducing its dependence on public funding, which – during his seven years in office he duly did – by cutting organisations in receipt of grants by half. Consequently, the second half of the eighties was largely dominated by the need to contract and retrench. Then, in 1994, the Arts Council of Great Britain was disbanded to enable the formation of separate arts councils for England, Scotland and Wales, a development that was to have profound consequences for the public support of the literatures of Wales.

Established in that year, the new Arts Council of Wales steadily gravitated towards an emphasis on the performing arts, partly because it was easier, under a new ideological dispensation inclined to view the arts merely as instruments of pleasure and entertainment, to justify significant spending in these publicly conspicuous areas. Internal reorganisation of the council also resulted in the replacement of art-specific departments (complete with specialist directors and committees) by flexible cross-cultural departments served by cognate advisors and committees. Particularly vulnerable in this new set-up were those core elements in the literature programme that concerned the publicly invisible but utterly indispensable processes of the production, marketing and sales of books. As the dependence of these on Arts Council funding came to seem increasingly anomalous, so a concerned Tony Bianchi – Senior Literature Officer of the old Welsh Arts Council who had stayed on as the sole literature specialist remaining within the Arts Council of Wales – began to explore the possibility of removing them from their precarious marginal context and transferring them to the care of the Welsh Books Council.

As discussions to this end drew to a successful conclusion, one element in the Arts Council's programme of literature support – the trade representation scheme designed to increase sales to bookshops of English-language books, and run in conjunction with a consortium of Welsh publishers – was transferred in advance to the Welsh Books Council. This provided the Books Council with a foretaste of the struggles ahead, with the immensely powerful leading chains of bookstores (Smiths, Waterstones, Borders) that could demand unconscionable discounts and were loath to adapt their central ordering schemes to cater for merely 'local' Welsh interests. Following the Kewley and Richardson review of the Welsh Books Council's trade representation service of July 2005 – that led to a major internal reorganisation of the sales and marketing arm of the Books Council – the scheme inherited from the Arts Council was replaced by an arrangement that charged regional reps with the responsibility of interesting bookshops in new titles both in Welsh and in English.

On April 1, 2003, much of the Arts Council of Wales's programme of support for the production of literature, along with the related funds, was transferred to the Welsh Books Council, with the Arts Council retaining only that residual element in the programme that related to the fostering and promotion (through public events) of contemporary authors. Originally 'delivered' by Academi (the revamped Welsh Academy of Writers), this 'rump' Arts Council of Wales programme of activities eventually became the preserve of Literature Wales. In the area of anglophone literature, the Books Council decided to ring-fence expenditure that had already been earmarked as block grants to revenue clients and major periodicals, or had been reserved for additional production grants of £117,752, author commission grants of £20,000 and magazine support at £7,000. The Council also decided to apply to these new funding initiatives the same criteria – stipulating literary merit rather than commercial viability – that had obtained while they were being managed by the Arts Council of Wales.

The incorporation of anglophone Welsh literature into a long-established programme of work, that had been designed exclusively to serve the needs of Welsh-speaking Wales, was a remarkably bold – and indeed culturally revolutionary – step by the Welsh Books Council, and would have been impossible but for the total dedication of its director, Gwerfyl Pierce Jones, to the realising of a dream of a genuinely bicultural Wales. And the challenging task of actually implementing this vision was entrusted, over the following decade, to a succession of outstanding English Grants Officers working in close conjunction with the lay members of the new Welsh Books Council panel established to manage this new development. Equally indispensable, of course, was the co-operation of an anglophone sector of the Welsh book world and publishing industry that had every historical reason to be mistrustful of an organisation 'distantly' located in what had long been perceived as the unofficial capital of the Welsh-language heartland, and that had hitherto been resolutely monocultural in all its operations. Moreover, the Books Council now found itself, through its anglophone publishing clients, operating not in a 'closed', local cultural context but in a fearsomely global and fiercely competitive publishing environment of which, hitherto, it had had no experience.

Nor were these the only challenges to be met. As Gwerfyl Pierce Jones noted in the inaugural meeting of the English Grants Panel, whereas the Arts Council of Wales's funding programme had been constrained by a brief to promote only 'literary excellence', the Welsh Books Council had from the outset seen it as part of its mission to strengthen the publishing industry in Wales. It had consequently always had to pay particular regard not only to cultural service but to commercial success. It seemed, therefore, as if this newly acquired programme of funding for anglophone 'literature' (as opposed to the more catholic designation of 'books' traditionally adopted in its very title by the Welsh Books Council) might end up occupying a position within the Council's operational plan almost as anomalous, and therefore as potentially precarious, as it had occupied within the Arts Council of Wales system.

Providentially, however, assistance to cut this Gordian knot was to come from a direction also, coincidentally, flagged up in the minutes of this inaugural meeting of the Council's English Grants Panel. Mention was there made of the National Assembly for Wales's ongoing policy review of English-medium writing in Wales, conducted under the auspices of its Culture, Welsh Language and Sport Committee. Following the devolution of limited powers of expenditure to the newly established National Assembly for Wales in 1997, it had taken responsibility first for funding the Arts Council of Wales and later (following pressing representations and the findings of the Task and Finish Group mentioned below) for funding the Welsh Books Council. By 2003, the Welsh-language publishing industry had benefited substantially from several new initiatives, introduced by the Books Council, that had been enabled by additional Welsh Assembly Government funding. The way had been prepared for this increase in financial support, by the report of a Welsh Assembly Government Task and Finish Group, chaired by Assembly Member Delyth Evans (2002) (on behalf of the then Minister for Culture, Sport and the Welsh Language, Jenny Randerson AM), that had highlighted the need for a raft of measures to improve the market appeal and commercial viability of Welsh-language books. Among those of the report's recommendations that were subsequently implemented by the Council, upon receipt of additional funding, were schemes to enable publishers to commission popular authors, to appoint creative editors and to construct more market-conscious revenue programmes. The net effect was a strengthening of the basic infrastructure of the Welsh-language sector of the publishing industry, and a professionalisation of its practices, very much along the lines that had been recommended in the Grant Thornton report on publication grants of 1999 and highlighted in a comprehensive and ambitious strategy document co-ordinated by the Council, *Working Together: Publishing in Welsh with the Support of the Publishing Grant: a Five-year Strategy* (2000).

Conscious of having created, through these important measures, a significant imbalance between public provision in the Welsh- and English-language publishing sectors, and following strong lobbying from the Books Council, the National Assembly's Culture Committee instituted the policy review into anglophone literary culture mentioned above, and duly invited representations from a number of key individuals and organisations including the Books Council. The ensuing report was published in March 2004, and its core recommendations were reflected in the important announcement of Culture Minister Alun Pugh in the autumn of that year of an additional quarter of a million pounds to be channelled into the anglophone publishing sector via the Books Council. This money was specifically designed to raise market awareness and to enhance the competitive capacity of Welsh anglophone publishers, with a view to improving the commercial performance of Welsh anglophone titles; and, in contrast to the literature grant inherited from the Welsh Arts Council, the emphasis was on enabling reasonable commercial success within what was readily acknowledged to be the most formidably resistant of global markets.

There were four important new transformative initiatives enabled by this additional sum of money. The first was an author advance scheme, 'to allow publishers to invest in a wider range of more popular titles which are likely to raise revenue through sales, which will in turn allow the publishers to invest further in their infrastructure and other titles of Welsh interest and literary merit.' Criteria for awards under this scheme related not only to quality but to commercial potential. Second was a new marketing scheme, that in practice attempted to implement several of the key findings of the groundbreaking joint marketing strategy of October 2003. The need for such a strategy had been one of the recommendations of the Welsh Assembly Government's Task and Finish Group (2002) and the production of the strategy was co-ordinated by the Books Council. This scheme was designed to complement the author advance scheme by making sums available for publicity campaigns aimed at fulfilling the sales promise of the titles the latter scheme had funded. Thirdly, there was the supported posts scheme, designed to enable publishers to appoint editors who would work on enhancing both the quality and marketability of their books. Finally, a trade awards scheme would allow the Council to reward outstanding achievements by publishers in such key related areas as production values and sales performance.

In addition to these, the Books Council was charged, under this new funding arrangement, with the management of a new prestigious Library of Wales scheme to bring classics back into print, building on the foundations laid by publishers such as Seren and Honno. Placed from the outset under what proved to be the outstanding general editorship of Dai Smith, the Library was to be produced by a publisher to be appointed for what turned out to be a series of fixed franchise periods, by public tender. The initial cultural significance of this heritage initiative outstripped even its impressive subsequent performance under the Parthian imprint, with titles produced eventually numbering 50. and sale figures buoyant. Modelled on the great modern Library of America, the Library of Wales, theatrically launched with much fanfare both in Wales and in New York, was consciously conceived, from the outset, as a belated public acknowledgement by an avowedly bicultural nation of its great pride in its anglophone literary inheritance. The Library was an ambitious exercise in the transmission of culture, and its inauguration furnished a dramatic instance of the identity politics being practised by a fledgling, nation-building Assembly. It was a development publicly endorsed, in due course, by the First Minister, Rhodri Morgan, as the single most important initiative of his long formative period in office.

The receipt, from two such different sources, of two substantial sums for English-language book production, to which two contrasting sets of obligations and criteria were attached, naturally dictated that the Books Council adopt a delicate twin-track policy in this important new anglophone area of its operations. In so doing, however, it acted as much from cultural conviction as from mere expediency. In the one context, it continued to apply an evaluative term ('literature') that had for some time been treated as problematic but that nevertheless continued to be culturally indispensable. In the other context, it employed the more neutrally descriptive term 'books', but was then still faced with having to make evaluative distinctions. It did so by applying the hospitably flexible criterion of 'quality of writing', that had the incidental advantage of also being applicable in the other, 'literary', context.

There was, however, no doubt, that with the injection of a whole new exciting dynamic into the Books Council's proceedings by the acquisition of the Welsh Assembly Government's new grant, the primary thrust of the Council's work in the area of anglophone book production was hereafter to be in the direction of identifying, producing, marketing and selling books of what the minister Alun Pugh termed 'wide popular appeal'. This, in turn, meant assisting experienced, talented, creatively inventive and enthusiastic publishers to equip themselves to compete, on tolerably equal terms, in what was acknowledged to be an extremely difficult global market, one tiny inseparable corner of which was the 'home' market of Wales itself.

Improved market performance obviously both required and stimulated an expansion in the 'production base'. In other words, as books not only increased in number but sought to satisfy extensively varied demand, so the number of publishers needed to produce them was likely to increase. At the time of takeover from the Arts Council of Wales, only two publishers of English-language books (Seren and Gomer) were entrusted with block grants that allowed them to construct their own annual publishing programmes without substantial reference to the English Grants Panel, a step towards maturity and, hypothetically, towards self-sufficiency. The extension of the block grants scheme over the coming years to include Honno and Parthian was a measure of the striking advances made by the Welsh publishing industry under this new dispensation. Parallel to this was to be the arrival of significant new players on the English-language publishing scene, including Cinnamon, Accent, Graffeg, Carreg Gwalch and Y Lolfa (previously almost exclusively a prominent Welsh-language publisher). These were reliant on an individual book grants scheme which allowed for considerable flexibility of product since it did not make awards dependent on the demonstrably high commercial potential of titles.

Welsh publishers had long been disadvantaged by being skeletal operations, financially unable to afford the teams of specialist staff that were the industry standard elsewhere. The supported posts scheme was accordingly a modest attempt to remedy a deficiency that had often prevented publishers from constructing, managing and delivering commercially competitive publishing programmes. By enabling publishers to appoint editors, for example, the scheme aimed not only at improving the quality of basic text production (copy editing) but also at spotting market trends and helping authors fashion texts of quality and commercial viability (creative editing). And recognising that constrained circumstances had in the past discouraged Welsh publishers from looking beyond the production of the printed page to the process of marketing (and therefore selling) the finished article, the new scheme enabled them to add dedicated marketing specialists to their staff. Further acknowledging that individual publishers still lacked the resources to mount the kind of marketing campaigns needed to make an impact on influential media outlets, the Council instituted its own publicists scheme. Experienced specialist companies were appointed, for a fixed term, to promote books selected from the whole 'stable' of Welsh anglophone publishers to the media both in London and in Wales.

Such initiatives not only recognised the need to prioritise market performance but highlighted the dependence of sales and marketing on the prompt, reliable advance provision of pre-publication data, much of it by electronic means. They also stressed strict adherence to publication dates chosen very much with an eye on peak seasonal opportunities. These were some of the issues that had been constructively addressed in the Kewley and Richardson review of the Books Council's trade representation scheme (July 2005), a major document that resulted in a radical restructuring both of the Council's own Sales and Marketing Department and a change in the relationship in these areas between the Council and its independent publishing partners. In essence, publishers were given the option of choosing between three levels of service offered by the Council, from straightforward wholesaling through to an exclusive distribution contract. In parallel with this went a new requirement that publishers conform to best professional trade practice by ensuring greatly improved information flows up and down the supply chain. The whole of the Kewley-Richardson report was based on the premise that 'under the right circumstances, and with appropriate funding and professional guidance there is considerable growth potential for Welsh books in both languages'. The challenging implications of that encouraging statement were not lost on the Council and its partners.

Ever conscious of the advantages, in some areas, of centrally supporting initiatives it would not be cost-effective for individual publishers to undertake, the Books Council began to institute an occasional series of seminars, open to all its partners, addressing important aspects of author relations, text production, design, marketing and sales. These were conducted by professionals who had extensive experience of operating at the very heart of the commercial environment in which Welsh publishers were competing. And also conscious that the industry would in due course be held accountable by the Welsh Assembly Government, in terms measured for the most part by improved sales performance, for the success of the generous new funding schemes from which the Welsh publishing sector was benefiting, the Council, through its English Grants Panel, began to agree a number of targets and performance indicators with its partners which would allow it to monitor the efficacy of its various innovations. These agreed outcomes would be regularly reviewed by the panel in the context of the other steps it simultaneously set in place to ensure effective management of its funding programme. They included annual reviews by panel members of the publishing programmes of its revenue clients, panel interviews with representatives of each of its publishers in turn, and regular officer consultations with publishers, supplemented by annual meetings that allowed exchange of views in the light of panel comments on their respective records.

The panel also instituted in-house measures to encourage commercial performance. Marketing grants were closely tied to an author advance scheme where awards were made dependent on credible forecasts of strong sales; bonuses were awarded for meeting agreed advance publication dates during peak purchasing seasons such as Christmas; penalties were levied for missing crucial production dates during these same periods; and in due course, revenue publishers were required to ensure that their publication programme, in any given year, featured a set of predicted strong sellers that could, if necessary, offset titles (otherwise valuable or even prestigious) whose sales potential might be less impressive. It also became apparent to the panel that while websites not only showcased products but were also becoming important points of sale, its publishing partners were experiencing difficulties in keeping abreast of developments in this remarkably quick-moving scene. Accordingly, it made one-off grants available for the professional upgrading of sites.

One of the recommendations in the National Assembly's policy review of English-medium Writing in Wales had been that 'Library authorities, in conjunction with the Books Council, should consider ways of improving, sourcing and purchasing Welsh Writing in English.' Implicit in this was the recognition that this body of writing had hitherto received very little public exposure in the very country that had produced it and whose condition it had been concerned to address. What was also implicitly recognised was that a vicious circle existed, whereby lack of exposure led to ignorance which in turn led to lack of informed library staff able to remedy the lack of exposure. This was a circle that could be broken only through the intervention of a sympathetic and informed outside body.

Accordingly, the Council commissioned a report from D. Hywel E. Roberts on 'Improving the Sourcing and Purchasing of Welsh Writing in English in Libraries in Wales in conjunction with the Welsh Books Council'. One of its key recommendations, duly implemented with the ready support of CyMAL, the policy division of the Welsh Government responsible for museums, archives and libraries' services, was that 'a core list of Welsh Writing in English titles should be created and disseminated annually to public libraries in Wales to assist them to improve their sourcing and purchasing policies,' and that the Welsh Books

Council should be invited to advise on the construction of such a list. As Roberts made clear, this recommendation was predicated on the assumption (subsequently proved to be correct) that when the standards framework for Welsh libraries was next reviewed in 2005, it would place libraries under a statutory requirement to ensure they annually sourced and purchased a select core stock of Welsh writing in English titles. Consequent to this, a requirement of the Council to 'assist libraries to source and acquire titles' was included in the remit letter sent in February 2005 by the then Minister for Culture, Welsh Language and Sport, Alun Pugh, and reiterated the following year.

To view the recommendations of the Roberts report as peripheral to the essential work of the English Grants Panel would be a serious error. Since borrowers constitute a significant proportion of book readers, libraries are well positioned to bring the products of the Welsh publishing industry to public attention. And their contribution in this regard is all the more vital because (as is further noted below) there are pitifully few other opportunities of this invaluable kind 'naturally' and routinely available. It was all the more dismaying, therefore, when cutbacks in local authority funding resulted in the removing from library authorities of the legal obligation to buy even a small sample of anglophone Welsh titles.

As the case of the libraries clearly demonstrates, books are not produced, nor do they exist, in a social vacuum. They are given living currency in our lives and realise their potential through being part of what might be termed the 'conversation of culture' in both its 'high' and 'popular' forms; and insofar as that conversation relates to the book world, it relies in significant part on symposia such as journals, magazines and periodicals to sustain it. Moreover, these publications are central to Wales's maintenance of that intellectual conversation with itself and with the outside world upon which it, like every other civilised country, depends for its meaningful existence. Equally importantly, they provide a plurality of creative talents, both established and emergent, with opportunities for showcasing their work. Consequently, the English Grants Panel has always been very appreciative of the publications franchise it inherited from the Arts Council of Wales, recognising not least the symbiotic and synergistic relationship between periodicals and all the other elements in its overall funding programme.

Following the transfer of the magazine funding programme to its care in 2003, the Council retained the pattern of franchises it had inherited from the Arts Council of Wales for a further decade. This arrangement provided for one journal addressing the interests of Wales's anglophone literary culture, one wide-ranging journal engaging with key economic, social, political and cultural issues of the day, and one magazine devoted to the poetry scene at home and beyond. At the end of each franchise period, these periodicals repeatedly attracted accolades from independent external assessors who not only commented favourably on production values that rivalled the best the London scene had to offer, but also emphasised the strength of sales relative to the scale of the home market.

But, impressive as well as culturally invaluable though the performance of the long-term holders of the publications franchise continued to be, it eventually became apparent that despite their very best efforts they were struggling to adapt to the startling new exigencies, and ambivalent opportunities, created by the digital age. Between 2006 and 2012, sales declined by almost 30%. Concern about what was by then already an evident downward turn was voiced by Alun Ffred Jones, the then Heritage Minister, in his remit letter of March 2009 instructing the Council to 'ensure that [English-language magazines] enhance and diversify [their] content … and increase their market reach, including exploiting the opportunities provided by new technology.' This was a challenge the English Grants Panel consistently drew to the attention of the journal editors, who responded with a variety of vigorous and enterprising marketing strategies, many of them involving the spectrum of social media and digital platforms. The marginal success of these intensified panel concerns, voiced with particular urgency during the review process that terminated each three-year franchise period. Nevertheless, sales figures continued to show relatively little improvement, so that it became increasingly difficult to demonstrate value for money. In the light of these worrying developments, the panel made some pragmatic adjustments to the established franchise system in order to free up funds to accommodate new clients with wider agendas, in the hope of attracting new cohorts of readers.

However, such remedies proved insufficient, and so in 2012, the Council commissioned an independent review of English-language magazines in Wales, guided by up-to-date market research. In spring 2014, the three-person review team, chaired by Tony Bianchi, submitted a thoroughgoing report for the Council's attention, which roundly concluded that 'the current position of English-language cultural magazines is not sustainable.' Among the reasons for this, it noted, were 'poor and declining value for money' (largely owing to decline in sales) and 'uncertainties about the digital future' that represented a 'threat to print'. It recommended that the Council consider adopting one of the three viable alternative models it proposed, common to which were such key innovations as 'maximum gearing ratio (i.e. proportion of grant to generated income) for each print title supported', and a definition of 'magazine' that was 'as fluid and as non-prescriptive as possible with regard both to format and subject-matter.' It also emphasised the need to ensure investment in 'innovative digital options'.

On the advice of its English Grants Panel, the Council adopted a mixed programme of funding for print and digital productions, some of which would concentrate on one or more of the traditional genres of literature, while others would 'span a number of areas including current affairs, politics, history, economics, the arts, culture (including popular culture), media, the environment, sport and leisure.' Seed funding was also made available to encourage innovative short-term experiments that could result in future major developments.

No more dismaying instance could be found of a longstanding imbalance between the Welsh-language and the English-language sides of the Books Council's operations than in the striking difference in the number and the quality of the books available for children and young readers. The wealth of Welsh-language books produced, notable both for variety of content and high production values, served only to underline the paucity of English-language provision. Such a disparity between the two language sectors was deeply regrettable, not least because of its implications for the future of Welsh anglophone culture. Until very recently, the only books addressing their own local experience that non Welsh-speaking youngsters in Wales could turn to were those available in the admirable, pioneering Pont series produced by Gomer. Then in 2013, following representations from the Council, the then Minister for Culture, Huw Lewis, released a small additional, non-recurrent sum sufficient for a two-year pilot scheme aimed at launching two new 'series', one of five fiction titles for children between seven and nine, the other of five non-fiction titles for those from nine to eleven. No sooner was the first tranche of books published, however, than funding cuts virtually ruled out any possibility of continuing what promised to be a highly successful, and very important, experiment. Moreover, with the probable demise of the scheme came a serious threat to Firefly, one of the two publishing companies involved, newly formed by enthusiasts with the express purpose of producing attractive anglophone books for Welsh children. The crisis was a harsh reminder of how important an indirect contribution the Books Council had for years been making to steadily extending the portfolio of small businesses within the Welsh economy, most particularly those situated in economically underdeveloped areas. The termination of this short-lived scheme served only to underline the poignancy of an observation recorded in the foreword to the 2004 National Assembly report on Welsh writing in English. It is the wish of the Culture, Welsh Language and Sport Committee, wrote the chairman, Rosemary Butler, 'that Welsh Writing in English [be] studied as widely as possible in our education system.' The pilot scheme inaugurated by Huw Lewis had briefly seemed to promise first steps in the direction of introducing youngsters of primary school age to books about their own place and country, and in enabling the appearance of Firefly, which has gone from strength to strength, its long-term value evident.

The fate of that short-lived scheme also highlighted another potential problem. That was recent government practice of directing significant additional funds away from the baseline provision upon which all the core operations of the Council depended, and that sustained the infrastructure without which, as had been emphasised in the authoritative Grant Thornton Report of the nineties, the publishing industry in Wales could not function. New expenditure increasingly tended to come in the form of non-recurrent funding for Government-specified new initiatives.

There was much to be said for the latter approach. It made for valuable experiment, flexibility and innovation, and it incidentally enabled the Council to diversify the sources of its public income, since government departments other than that of Culture (historically the exclusive sponsor of its activities) had begun to avail themselves of its services. In turn, the Council began to make substantial contributions to a variety of important fields such as those of literacy (the domain of the Education Department) and social justice (through Reading Communities projects in deprived areas), and also successfully fostered a wider reading culture through the range of activities linked annually to the celebration of World Book Day. An important by-product of this government shift towards project-based funding was the formation by the Council of fruitful partnerships with a range of other public sector bodies.

It was this new dispensation of short-term funding that also enabled the Council to secure several timely one-off grants in rapidly developing digital fields such as e-publishing. While developments in this crucial new area are addressed in depth in another chapter, it is worth noting here in passing that seed-corn Welsh Government funding has allowed the Council to assist publishers both to produce more than a thousand e-books to date.

But for each of these undoubted gains there has also been a serious corresponding risk, because the greater the proportion of the Books Council's grant supplied in this far-flung, ad hoc, occasional and non-recurrent fashion, the greater the likelihood that a council correspondingly starved of new money for core services will face difficulty in protecting, let alone enhancing, activities that are not only foundational to its own existence but essential for the well-being of the publishing industry reliant upon its grants and services.

Problems, too, as well as opportunities, have resulted – most particularly for Welsh writing in English – from the tendency to link grants ever more directly to market performance. Setting aside the evidently huge challenges associated with competing in the vast global market for English-language books, much more thought needs to be given to the mindset of the readers that have long constituted the anglophone book market in Wales. That mindset was the manifestation of a congeries of settled, socially determined habits of taste and preference born of an accumulation of experiences. The deep problem for the Welsh book industry was that anglophone readers were likely to have little instinctive interest in Welsh books because they had so rarely come across them either in their formative years or as adults. Consequently, such books could paradoxically seem like suspect unfamiliar products. So when it came to buying, readers rarely, if ever, 'thought Welsh' (as opposed to strictly 'local') except perhaps in the case of niche (though popular) interests such as sport. The result was that a distinctively 'Welsh' book market had had very little encouragement in the past to develop and was still at an embryonic stage of growth.

To make public support for the Welsh book industry too directly conditional on the performance of books in that particular market would therefore be ill-advised. Despite the huge advances made over a decade of substantial investment, the market for anglophone Welsh books continues to contrast depressingly with that, say, for 'local' products in contemporary Scotland or Ireland. It is a decades-old dilemma with complex socio-political roots and could be remedied only slowly through the steady implementation, over a long period of time, of a 'holistic' approach. This would involve fundamental innovations (requiring appropriate funding) in a whole range of interrelated fields, from education through bookshops to the media, both traditional and digital. A mature anglophone Welsh book market needs to be carefully 'grown' before it can be exploited, and it remains an important part of the Books Council's work, through its publishing partners and bookshop outlets, to encourage such a growth.

Curtailment of funding can have unforeseen implications. Small enhancements of the budget have always made a huge difference to the internal economy of the Welsh book industry, but so also do small reductions. Damage can very easily and quickly be done to a delicate ecosystem that it has taken years to construct and that relies, for effective operation, on a complex of interdependent activities. It is vital that under the pressure of current economic difficulties we do not lose such ground (dramatically substantial by historic Welsh standards) as has, over the past decade, been gained.

There are even less obvious dangers. Minutely examine any English-language book with a Welsh provenance or dimension and you will almost certainly detect, hidden away among the clutter of the front-matter such as the ISBN that no one reads, the modest legend 'published with the assistance of the Welsh Books Council'. It takes eyesight of almost microscopic keenness to discover it. The Council undoubtedly has an image problem, which is most pronounced in the context of Welsh anglophone culture. Whereas a promotional agency may, inadvertently or otherwise, promote itself in the very act of promoting a client, and thus press its claim to continued public funding, a service agency (which is what the Council is in essence), is prevented by the very nature of its largely covert operations from attracting much attention to itself. In making itself indispensable, it is also in danger of making itself self-effacingly invisible. And in a market-obsessed era in which establishing a strong 'brand' identity is increasingly important, the consequence of a lack of assertive profile may in future prove seriously damaging when it comes to competing for shrinking sums of public money.

And then there is the threat that stems from Wales's historic and continuing failure to measure its needs by any yardstick other than that which lies so beguilingly ready to hand in the example of Anglo-American practice. This is a threat that may keenly impact on the future of public subsidy of anglophone Welsh publications. With England following the US lead and opting increasingly to entrust book production entirely to the play of market forces, for how long will Wales be able to resist following suit, however tentatively, if pressures continue to build on the public purse? Ignorance of, or indifference to, instructive other cases much more cognate with its own, may well facilitate the development. Who in Wales has bothered to examine the measures that anglophone Canada has consistently taken, for example, to defend itself against the otherwise irresistible power of the neighbouring US market? There, 'the federal government's Book Publishing Industry Development Program with a budget of over $3 million, helps the Canadian publishing industry produce and promote Canadian-authored books domestically and internationally'.[1] And such initiatives are commonplace across the anglophone world from Canada to New Zealand.

Notwithstanding a rolling programme of notable initiatives, the 2010s proved to be a decade of strategic survival for the Books Council (not unlike that faced by the Welsh Arts Council in the 1980s, documented above). The Conservative Westminster governments of that decade sought to mitigate the effects of the financial downturn inaugurated by the 'crash' of 2008 by initiating a programme of financial austerity whose effects would be felt most devastatingly by the public sector. The willingness to unleash a period of economic instability following the

2016 referendum to leave the European Union, and the ability to find funds to sustain the furlough scheme and banking system during the Covid pandemic of 2020, has revealed that much of the austerity agenda had been ideological. This is of little compensation to the libraries closed in the previous decades. A series of dedicated Culture ministers and their deputies have, however, overseen the Welsh Government's defence of the publishing sector, and enabled the Books Council to introduce a raft of new programmes, under the imaginative leadership of a new chief executive officer, Helgard Krause.

The predicted obsolescence of print media in the face of digital publishing has proved premature, though the disappearance of some bookshops from the high streets of Wales in the face of online purchasing has been detrimental to society's awareness of the publishing industry. The Books Council of Wales has responded to this challenge by investing in a new digital system to manage the sale, supply and distribution of books and by re-vamping Gwales, its online book ordering service. The civic frame created by an evolving Welsh polity has allowed the internal diversity of Wales to be expressed in ways beyond that of language, with new literary voices emerging from the nation's BAME and LGBTQ communities. In recent years, the Books Council has collaborated with the Reading Agency and the Welsh Government in developing 'reading on prescription' and 'iechyd da' schemes, increasing the availability of books in the case of the former, and encouraging children to understand and discuss issues around health and wellbeing in the latter.

The Covid pandemic of 2020–2021 has presented the Council with perhaps the greatest challenges it has had to face during its entire existence, and it has served as the most severe stress-test exercise that could have been imagined. Throughout this period, the reliance of the publishing industry in Wales on Welsh Government funding, all provided, managed and channelled by the Council, has been extremely apparent. It is very much to the credit of that government that it has supplied the Council with additional funds that enabled it to adjust and innovate in a variety of ways that have assisted writers, publishers and small bookshops throughout the country to survive. And, thanks to the dedication and the flexibility of the staff, major new developments have been introduced, such as the radical revamping of Gwales and its large portfolio of platforms and services, the reconfiguration of the Council's internal management structure, and the provision online of an app facilitating the production of e-books. Consequently, as Wales emerges from the COVID pandemic, the Books Council is well positioned to respond to the nation's growing diversity, and to engage with the increasingly central issues of mental health and wellbeing.

Sixty years after its foundation, the Books Council has therefore developed into a seminal institution capable of serving a nation whose writers so strongly identify as bicultural that we almost require a new word – ambicultural, perhaps – to signify their passionate sense of being equally fulfilled by, and equally committed to, creative expression in both Welsh and English. Perhaps the most brilliant exemplar of this phenomenon is Gwyneth Lewis, who has written:

> Lord of the Running Rivers,
> I was given two languages
> To speak or, rather, they have spoken me
> Through different landscapes from a common spring.

It is the privilege of the Books Council of Wales, in its new, augmented, incarnation, to serve the vibrant publishing industry of a country characterised by two linguistic landscapes that are fruitfully different in character, but which are both watered from 'a common spring' of Welsh identity.

Professor M. Wynn Thomas recently took up a new position (following the Council's restructuring as a charitable incorporated organisation in April 2021) as Chair of the Board of Trustees of the Books Council of Wales. Prior to that he had been Chair of the Council for some years. He is also Professor of English and Emyr Humphreys Chair of Welsh Writing in English at Swansea University, and is the former Director and founder of CREW (the Centre for Research into the English Literature and Language of Wales).

Note

[1] Jocelyn Harvey, 'Arts, Heritage and Cultural Industries funding,' at http://www.thecanadianencyclopedia.ca/en/article/arts-heritage-and-cultural-industries-funding/ (accessed August 19, 2014).

Appealing to the Young

*Publishing for children
and young people*

Appealing to the Young

*D. Geraint Lewis on publishing
for children and young people*

For centuries, the child in Wales had been treated as a young adult with a soul to be saved. But by the end of the nineteenth century, the Nonconformist denominations were more aware of the needs of children and of the need to provide suitable reading matter for them. Each of the four denominations in Wales had its own Bookroom, with publishing and distribution divisions, issuing both books and magazines. At its peak, the magazine *Trysorfa y Plant* (The Children's Treasury), founded in 1862, sold around forty thousand copies a month across all denominations.

By the end of the nineteenth century, a new cause had emerged, that of education. As chief inspector of the Board of Education in Wales from 1907 to 1920, O.M. Edwards worked tirelessly to ensure that every child in Wales should receive a suitable education, including being educated in Welsh. He founded the magazine *Cymru'r Plant* (Children's Wales), begun in 1892, which published the early work of numerous authors, and ultimately brought about the transformation of Welsh literature for children, in terms of its content and style.

In 1927, the Board of Education published *Welsh in Education and Life*.[1] This contains a wide-ranging and inclusive review of social and educational developments in relation to the Welsh language through the centuries, with a particular emphasis on the state of Welsh education in the first quarter of the twentieth century. Yet despite its range of vision and bold words, the report contained virtually nothing about Welsh books for adults, and its messages regarding children's books were mixed. Though it paid tribute to the work of O.M. Edwards, the report's call for a broader range of reading books would be undermined by comments such as: 'We believe that there is a tendency to place too great an emphasis on the shortage of suitable books.'[2] It is perhaps no surprise that the report's recommendations were not implemented.

A new Education Act came into force in 1944, and Cardiganshire was one of the counties which responded enthusiastically to the opportunities it created. Alun R. Edwards describes how the county library service set about flooding its small schools with colourful books. But they were books in English , and some head teachers would refuse to receive the library van when it visited. As we have seen in a previous chapter, he was accused by one headmistress of killing children's appetite for reading Welsh and was badly shaken by the realisation that he of all people could be contributing to the death of the Welsh language.[3]

Something had to be done, and in 1951, Alun Edwards recalls that the proceedings of the county Education Committee turned into a 'Revivalist meeting', where it was decided to establish a Welsh Books Committee with the authority to spend £2,000 in a financial year to promote writing, illustrating and publishing Welsh books for children. His pragmatic comment at the time was: 'Writing books for children under eight years old is neither an art nor a miracle. It is business.'[4] It must be said that many of Alun R. Edwards's new ideas were brought to fruition through the county Education Committee, and without the support of its enlightened director of education, Dr John Henry Jones, it is unlikely that these revolutionary schemes would have seen the light of day.

The state of Welsh-language book publishing was parlous: only six books for children appeared in 1945, and R.E. Griffith, Secretary of the Union of Welsh Publishers and Booksellers, was convinced that the demise of publishing in Welsh was imminent, owing to paper rationing and the lack of any grants to produce suitable books for schools.[5] The union decided to take the contentious step of appealing to the government for support for Welsh books.[6] In terms of children's books, the only silver thread running through the darkness of these years was the work of Urdd Gobaith Cymru (The League of Welsh Youth). Ifan ab Owen Edwards had inherited the editorship of *Cymru'r Plant* from his father; there was also *Yr Aelwyd* (The Hearth), a magazine for young people, and *Young Wales*, an English-language quarterly. The Urdd was also responsible for organising and administering book campaigns which succeeded in selling over 200,000 books in a ten year period.[7]

In response to the appeal of the Union of Welsh Publishers and Booksellers, the Home Office established a committee to investigate publishing in Welsh and to report on measures for supplying the needs of schools and colleges and the Welsh-speaking populace. Reference has been made elsewhere in this volume to the work of the Ready committee.[8] In this context it is worth noting that the committee rejected the approach taken by Cardiganshire to resolve the problem of a lack of children's books[9] (doubts were cast on the Education Committee's authority to spend money in such a way), and the Ready committee recommended the establishment of a new body to administer 'the Welsh Books Foundation' which would purchase and supply Welsh books to education authorities.[10] This was another recommendation that was never implemented.

The Welsh Joint Education Committee had been established in 1948 as a joint board of the Welsh education authorities. The WJEC already had a panel which advised publishers on the suitability of authors' manuscripts for schools, and as a result of the Ready committee recommendation, this grew into a Welsh books sub-committee, which succeeded in persuading fifteen of the seventeen education authorities then existing to spend a specific minimum on Welsh books for schools every year. At the same time, the Cardiganshire scheme continued in parallel with that of the WJEC. The essence of this scheme was that each county was responsible for recognising the needs of its schools and for finding new material for children's books – either through competitions to encourage and stimulate authors, or by commissioning books which the counties would undertake to purchase in agreed numbers. Under Alun Edwards's enthusiastic leadership, the one county scheme became a seven-county scheme, and in 1964 Anglesey, Caernarfonshire, Cardiganshire, Flintshire, Merionethshire, Montgomeryshire and Pembrokeshire transferred the scheme to the WJEC. By 1975, a catalogue was issued listing over 600 Welsh-language books for children which were still in print.[11] In 1976, on the basis of an analysis of publishing for children in minority languages, the publisher Roger Boore noted that 119 children's books had been published in a year under the WJEC scheme. In his opinion, 150 Welsh books were needed annually to meet the reading needs of children: it was therefore a 'considerable achievement' to reach 119.[12] This programme delivered books for learners as well as for native Welsh speakers, while Welsh-language course textbooks were also produced. The pattern of county competitions, under the aegis of the WJEC, led to considerable activity and a wide variety of authors and materials. Editorial officers were appointed to the Welsh Department of the WJEC, and, most importantly, the books were published by commercial publishers, so enabling a publisher like Gwasg y Dref Wen to specialise in publishing books for children. The programme also ensured that the books would reach the schools where they were most needed.

Yet, in spite of the real strengths of the programme and its undoubted success, doubts were raised as to whether publishing Welsh books for children should be so inextricably linked to one scheme. Following the establishment of the College of Librarianship Wales in 1964, trainee librarians became thoroughly schooled in the field of children's books. With the reorganisation of local government in 1974, all the new large counties had professional librarians responsible for library services for children and schools. In that same year, a number of these librarians (myself included,) got together to form the Welsh Youth Libraries Association. There was unease about the design and content of the books published under the aegis of the WJEC, and authors and writers themselves were expressing doubts about the dilatoriness of the whole process. Moreover, 'Cymraeg Byw', a new, synthetic colloquial form of written Welsh for learners, was becoming so established that there was growing pressure to incorporate it into publications for native Welsh speakers. That pressure spread beyond the remit of the WJEC and its panels, to influence the Books Council itself, as well as the Urdd magazines. Doubts were being raised about the new forms of Welsh adopted, and the author T. Llew Jones railed against the use of 'Cymraeg Byw'.[13] It had indeed become the case that the emphasis in children's books was shifting from the child's interest in the subject matter, to the importance of the medium used. I can testify from personal experience that there was little voluntary reading of books in 'Cymraeg Byw' in Cardiganshire schools, where Welsh was a first language.

In addition to the WJEC and the Welsh Books Council, one of the most influential bodies dealing with literature in Wales in both Welsh and English was the Welsh Arts Council. Under the leadership of the dynamic head of its Literature

Department, Meic Stephens, it was intent on changing the face of publishing in Wales. It grant aided the Welsh Books Council to establish professional Design and Editorial Departments to support the work of small presses and publishers, and it also supported the promotion of books and literature.

The Literature Department was totally focused on material for adults until, in 1974, one of the members of the Literature Committee produced a bombshell review of the state of Welsh publishing for children. Mairwen Gwynn Jones was the author of the comprehensive and far-reaching report *Llenyddiaeth i Blant yng Nghymru* (Literature for Children in Wales),[14] which was the most articulate expression of the unease that was gathering about the situation regarding books for children in Wales. The author states:

> It could be said, in sum, that the missing element from the standpoint of young Welsh readers is the sheer joy of books. One reason for this at present is that the 'business' of Welsh books for children is too closely tied up with the education system.[15]

She went on to list what would become a work programme for children's books outside the education sphere for the following twenty years:

1. Establish annual prizes for the author and illustrator of the best book for children
2. Start a children's book club in Welsh
3. Produce travelling exhibitions
4. Promote author visits to schools and foster the craft of storytelling
5. Prepare a plan to entice children and parents to buy books
6. Start a Children's Bulletin
7. Review children's books seriously
8. Establish a federation for activities and discussion of children's literature
9. Organise a weekend school in the form of a 'Literary Conference' with authors, publishers, reviewers and educationalists etc. dealing with books for children
10. Persuade the media to give greater attention to children's books in their programmes
11. Set aside one day of the year for a Children's Books Festival
12. Produce a magazine of nursery age stories.[16]

The report was approved by the Arts Council Literature Committee and, in 1976, in order to implement some of the recommendations, a new Children's Literature

Panel, chaired by Mairwen Gwynn Jones, was established. The panel could spend its budget on activities other than books, on condition that such activities were a means of promoting children's literature. As far as books were concerned, a decision was taken to concentrate on producing a small number of original and colourful books of a high literary standard, ambitious in content and design. As they would be costly to produce, these volumes would have to be published over a long period and paid for from more than one year's budget.

Frank Keyse, the children's book specialist at the College of Librarianship Wales, responded to the first recommendation of the report with a paper to the Welsh Youth Libraries Association outlining the need for a prize 'for original works published in Wales in the Welsh Language'.[17] At a meeting held in 1975 between librarians, the Arts Council and the WJEC, it was decided to establish two prizes, one for an original book in Welsh and the other for a book in English relating to Wales. Meic Stephens's suggestion of the name Tir na n-Og Awards was accepted. Half the Welsh prize was funded by the WJEC and the other half, and the whole of the English prize, by the Welsh Arts Council. The prize would be administered by the Welsh Youth Libraries Association.

It can be seen in retrospect that two contrasting elements were at work here. The first was the need to raise the status of authors of children's books in Welsh, and the second was the desire – and duty in the eyes of the prize's founders – to raise the standard of Welsh books by taking a critical look at publishers' output from year to year. It was T. Llew Jones, first winner of the Welsh Tir na n-Og Award, who drew attention to this uneasy marriage in a memorable address when accepting the award and lambasting the organisers for undermining his good name as an author in the public process of assessing the books. The following year, the new Children's Literature Panel of the Welsh Arts Council organised the prizes, while the librarians were responsible for selecting the winning volumes. As a result, the ceremony was far more ambitious and was held as the high point of a day of activities for children.

The year 1978 being the 'International Year of the Child', the Children's Literature Panel took advantage of the opportunity to press the Arts Council's Literature Committee for additional funding to establish a children's literature centre. The aim of the centre was to be a central repository for a substantial collection of material which would form the basis for the academic study of children's literature, as well as stimulating the development of creative writing for children and fostering an appreciation of children's literature in Wales. The College of Librarianship Wales made a bid to take responsibility for the proposed centre and a grant was awarded to the college to support the new institution.

A conference on children's books was established, the first held by the Arts Council in 1978. During subsequent years, specialist editors from English publishing houses were brought in to work with experienced Welsh authors such as Irma Chilton and Gwenno Hywyn, who then took responsibility for developing and training Welsh-language writers new to writing for children. Also in 1978, the Books Council received a grant from the Welsh Arts Council to publish *Sgwarnog*, a colourful magazine for children of primary age to promote books and reading in Welsh and English.

The same year saw the publication of *Cyhoeddi yn yr Iaith Gymraeg / Publishing in the Welsh Language* by the Council for the Welsh Language (an advisory body which reported to the Secretary of State).[18] This report enlarges on one of the principal recommendations of the Language Council, namely the need to 'develop in Wales an education system ... which can enable a person to read Welsh with pleasure at school and subsequently.'[19] It was recommended that:

> The Government grant should be increased ... to include ... leisure reading (outside the programmes of the Welsh Joint Education Committee) for children and young people ... a quarter of the total of this augmented grant should be dedicated to selected payments to support the production of reading materials in circles where demand is greatest.[20]

As a result, a new grant was established for the publishing of reading materials in Welsh for children and young people, and the Welsh Office invited the Books Council to be responsible for its distribution. The Council immediately set up panels to undertake the work: an Applications Panel to deal with the financial side, and a Children's Books Commissioning Panel, charged with identifying and filling gaps in the provision of leisure reading for children. One of the undoubted strengths of the Books Council has been its use of specialist panels to tackle the various aspects of its work. The willingness of busy, distinguished people to join these panels on a voluntary basis over the years is testimony to the acknowledged value of their work. Establishing panels was an opportunity to bring together the representatives of the WJEC and the Arts Council, along with librarians, authors, teachers and parents. Numerous schemes were instigated to produce a variety of appealing books, and programmes were shared between publishers according to their interests and their ability to complete the work.

This was the beginning of an exciting and lively time in the history of children's books. The WJEC reading scheme emphasised the needs of schools; the Arts Council's Literature Panel concentrated on a few ambitious and costly volumes, with a full programme of activities; and the Books Council was beginning to commission numerous volumes to fill gaps in children's leisure reading. The Commissioning Panel would meet overnight, and I recall electrifying meetings at which people who were passionate about children's books would draw on their experience and expertise to discuss plans and individual volumes, in the knowledge that their contribution would make a difference.

An encouraging development was the co-operation between organisations and publishers, fostered by the widely respected Books Council's Design Department. One thing that was not at issue was the standard of Welsh in the books produced. There were no complaints (in contrast to the days of Cymraeg Byw), thanks to the editorial departments of the various bodies. The pioneering work of the Editorial Department of Urdd Gobaith Cymru in this field should be acknowledged.

The link between the Children's Literature Centre and the College of Librarianship Wales came to an end in 1981. The Children's Literature Centre became an independent organisation under the aegis of the Arts Council and was relocated to the new headquarters of the Books Council. This was an opportunity for the Arts Council to transfer some of the responsibilities of its Children's Literature Panel to the Centre. From 1982, the centre was responsible for organising the Tir na n-Og awards and from 1985, it also took responsibility for the annual conference. In 1983, it received a grant to publish two new magazines, *Pori* (Browsing) and *Dragon's Tale*, with the aim of reviewing children's books and discussing developments in the field. In 1985, the centre established the Mary Vaughan Jones Award, to be presented every three years in recognition of an individual's contribution to children's books in Wales over a long period of time.

In addition to commissioning leisure reading for children, the Books Council oversaw a considerable increase in promotional activity in the field of children's books in this period. In 1983, the Council launched Clwb Sbondonics (The Sbondonics Club), to encourage children to buy books. Club members would receive a badge, a membership book, and a magazine – containing games, competitions and special prizes – on condition that they bought one book per term. The idea of a club caught on, and a display van, bought with a special grant from the Welsh Office, travelled around schools exhibiting the books available. Membership grew to almost 8,000, and acceptance of a book by Clwb Sbondonics guaranteed the publisher substantial sales. One result of the success of the club was that the magazine *Sgwarnog* was supplanted by the club magazine, and for a number of reasons, not least that it sought to include material for too wide a range of readers, *Sgwarnog* was discontinued.

A particular strength at this time was the growth of co-operation between the three organisations working in the field. For instance, when the Books Council's Commissioning Panel recognised the need for a series of leisure books which would appeal to readers aged from seven to nine, the Children's Literature Panel organised a course for editors and authors specialising in this area. The result was the series 'Cyfres Corryn'. When the WJEC established an ambitious series of historical novels, the Children's Literature Panel ensured that these novels should also be available in English, something which the WJEC could not do. And when the Books Council launched a series of novels for teenagers, the WJEC, which had a number of striking titles suitable for this age group, were happy to allow the series symbol to appear on their books. Another strength of these schemes was that they operated within a regime which respected the roles of author, publisher, Distribution Centre and bookshop, each an essential link in the process by which a book gets from author to reader.

Children's magazines had received little attention before the Books Council was granted new money by the Welsh Office. Before that, their production had been solely dependent on the Urdd and on a number of committed volunteers. An opportunity arose in 1980 to support the Urdd magazines, *Deryn* (Bird) and *Cymru'r Plant* to begin with, then from 1987, *Cip* (Glance), a fusion of the two. An interdenominational religious magazine for children, *Antur* (Adventure), in existence since 1966, received Books Council support until 1992. In 1949, the Bala artist and author, Ifor Owen, was privately publishing the comic *Hwyl* (Fun). This, the first – and indeed for many years the only – Welsh-language comic, did not receive public funding until 1980, when the Council offered it grant aid, it was to last another nine years, until the publisher's retirement.

Another wholly voluntary comic, one aimed at young boys, was *Hebog* (Hawk): sixty issues appeared between 1968 and 1973, edited by Gerallt Lloyd Owen. A change came when it was announced that there would be grant aid available from the Books Council for a new comic for children. Cyhoeddiadau Mei were commissioned to publish *Sboncyn* (Grasshopper), which appeared in 1980 as a lively new comic that caught the imagination of Welsh children. It achieved considerable popularity, selling over 7,000 copies a month, and was re-launched in 1988 under the name *Penbwl* (Tadpole), of which 73 issues appeared until its demise in 1995. The Council decided to re-tender for a comic for children, and from September 1996 to date has given its support to *Wcw* (Cuckoo), for three- to seven year-old-olds, which appears in association with the current affairs magazine *Golwg* (View). Between 1991 and the present day, there has also been Books Council support at various times for the teen magazines *Atolwg* and *V* (supplements to *Golwg*), *Sothach* (Rubbish, a pop magazine), *Tacsi* (Taxi), as well as for *Selar* (Cellar), published from 2004 to the present day, and, from 2019, *Lysh* (the latter, aimed at early teen girls, appears online and via social media). The comic *Mellten* was established in 2016, with Council support, published by Y Lolfa and edited by Huw Aaron, merging later on with *Cip*, which has currently moved online due to Covid restrictions. In separate ventures, some in partnership with S4C, others with individual presses or reflecting the passion of certain individuals such as Alun Ceri Jones of Dalen Press, there was a brief spate of comic-strip books (adaptations of TinTin and Asterix) and even graphic novels, such as *Y Mabinogi* (Hughes and Son, 2002).

Educational developments at this time saw the emergence of specialist centres such as the National Language Unit, the Religious Education Centre in Bangor and the Educational Resources Centre in Aberystwyth, which commissioned and produced educational materials for schools with the support of the Welsh Office. By now there were also developments in information technology, which enabled the production of specialist textbooks that could reach schools directly without the aid of publishers and traditional bookshops; for example, *Ystadegaeth Ragarweiniol: Tebygolrwydd a Theori Dosrannu* (Introductory Statistics: Probability and Distribution Theory), the first of this kind of textbook, published in 1984. Thus by the start of the 1990s, there was a strong, flexible and responsive infrastructure in place for producing, discussing and promoting children's books in Wales.

All this activity, and almost all of the twelve development points listed by Mairwen Gwynn Jones in 1974, were carried out during the time of Alun Creunant Davies at the Books Council's helm. However, it was the editorial and marketing head, and later deputy director of the Council, Gwerfyl Pierce Jones, who was chiefly responsible for leading the developments at the Books Council in the field of children's books (Gwerfyl became director of the Council in 1987: see her own chapter in this volume).

In 1990, at the request of the Welsh Arts Council, the Children's Literature Centre was incorporated into the Books Council: this was an opportunity to unite the promotional activities of the two bodies and to plan for the future. In taking over the centre, the Books Council inherited an extensive and valuable collection of children's books in Welsh and English. This material had been assembled as the core of an academic centre to enable the study of children's reading and children's literature, but as this was not a core function of the Books Council, a decision was taken to divide the collection in two. The unique and historical material was transferred to the National Library and other institutions concerned with teaching children's literature. The Welsh-language books were offered to the Education Department of the University College at Bangor and those in English to the English Department of the University College at Cardiff. Thanks to happy co-operation between the National Library of Wales, the Department of Library and Information Studies at University of Wales Aberystwyth, and the Books

Council, a comprehensive catalogue of Welsh-language children's books published between 1900 and 1991 was published.[21] That which remained in the care of the Council was a current collection of the output of the previous ten years, and with annual renewal, it would become the foundation of a colourful exhibition for teachers, librarians and anyone interested in children's books. The collection embodied the changes which had taken place in the world of children's books. By the 1990s, any collection of Welsh-language books for children could take its place alongside an equivalent English one in terms of quality of content and design. In ten years, a huge step forward had been made.

Another result of the rationalisation process within the new children's department was the discovery, through market research, that more copies of the Welsh Books Council's mainstream flagship periodical *Llais Llyfrau* were reaching Welsh schools than the specialist magazine *Pori*. It was a logical step, therefore, to include reviews of children's books and articles on matters relating to children's literature in *Llais Llyfrau,* both in Welsh and English, and to cease publishing *Pori* and *Dragon's Tale*.

With Welsh becoming a compulsory subject within the National Curriculum, the old Curriculum Council evolved in 1993 into the Curriculum and Assessment Authority for Wales (ACAC – or ACCAC by 1997) which was to take responsibility for the Welsh Curriculum. One of the roles which the Welsh Office transferred to the new body in 1995 was responsibility for commissioning material to support the teaching of Welsh as a subject and of other subjects taught through the medium of Welsh, along with bilingual (Welsh/English) materials to support the Welsh Curriculum. The process involved recognising what was needed and commissioning the material through competitive tender. Unlike the arrangements under the WJEC, the materials supported through ACCAC did not enjoy guaranteed sales, nor did they reach schools automatically. It was the responsibility of the publishers who won the tenders to market their materials to the schools. ACCAC was eager from the first to reinforce the efforts of publishers by availing itself of the marketing and central distribution programmes of the Books Council, and a close partnership was established between the two organisations. This was a means of ensuring that all Welsh schools knew what was available and how it could be ordered.

Indeed, ACCAC contributed money to develop some of the promotional programmes of the Books Council, not least the comprehensive catalogue which was sent annually to every school.

In 1991, following a visit by David Hunt, the Secretary of State for Wales, the Books Council received a grant to expand its schools programme to include a team of three officers, along with a co-ordinating officer at headquarters, who would visit schools to advise teachers on suitable materials and to process orders for them in co-operation with bookshops. Later ACCAC gave additional funding to employ another officer to strengthen the team.

Thanks to education programmes and the commissioning of leisure reading, there was now a greater variety of books available for children, schools and libraries; this period became a golden age for children's books. Clwb Sbondonics was very popular with children aged 7–11, and the next logical step was to found a similar club for children aged 3–7. Clwb Sbri-di-ri was founded in 1996, and proved just as popular. Authors and illustrators of children's books continued to be honoured, annually through the Tir na n-Og awards and every three years, through the Mary Vaughan Jones Award.

Hand in hand with the promotion of children's books, the promotion and encouragement of reading became an increasingly important part of the work of the Children's Books Department. Standards of reading and literacy being a matter of some concern in the field of education. With the exponential growth of television there was a genuine threat to children's reading habits, and as children who had not mastered the art of reading grew to adulthood and became parents who were unable to read, the problem was intensified. As a result, the government in London earmarked the year 1998–99 as the National Year of Reading throughout Britain. The Welsh Office invited the Books Council to lead a campaign in Wales, and Rhiannon Lloyd was appointed co-ordinator on secondment from Estyn (Her Majesty's Inspectorate of Education and Training in Wales). The year's main aims were:

- To raise the profile of reading in Wales
- To raise levels of attainment in reading and literacy
- To improve the literacy skills of children and of people in Wales generally
- To ensure a distinctive bilingual dimension to the year in Wales
- To enlist the support of every education authority

- To increase the sale of books
- To facilitate as many partnerships as possible.

The enthusiasm and successes of the year were captured in a report published in 1999.[23] Clearly, grass-roots activity sprang from a strong network of partnerships and effective co-operation between a very substantial number of bodies, movements and organisations. Yet the most striking indicator of the year's success was that the Assembly Government provided, from that point on, an annual grant for the organisation of a day every year to celebrate books and reading. Book Day has been an important event in the calendar of the book world ever since. In many ways, the Year of Reading was a turning point for the Council. Partnerships with various bodies to promote reading by children and adults, including a productive partnership with the Basic Skills Agency, were developed and enhanced.

1999 brought in the recognition of poets. In co-operation with the Welsh-language television channel S4C and Urdd Gobaith Cymru, the honorific post of Welsh-language Children's Laureate (Bardd Plant Cymru) was launched, spearheaded by Literature Wales. The aim was to raise the profile of poetry among young people and to encourage them to create and enjoy poetry. The first poet to grace the title was Myrddin ap Dafydd.

Meanwhile, during this same year came further developments in the ways that all books, including those for children, were promoted and critically received. The numbers reading *Llais Llyfrau* were declining, while the Gwales website was expanding. The work of reviewing books for adults, and those for children, including the output of the WJEC, was transferred to Gwales. Unlimited space was now available for reviews and the reviews were more timely and appeared more frequently. Inevitably it was decided that *Llais Llyfrau* should be discontinued.

As previously noted in this volume, the year 2002 was a critical year in the history of the Books Council. Following a detailed review by a panel set up by Jenny Randerson, the Minister for Culture, the Assembly Government acknowledged the need to increase grants substantially, and as a result there was an opportunity to invest more in the publishing industry and to place greater responsibility on the shoulders of the publishers. It was at this time that the Books Council, under the leadership of Gwerfyl Pierce Jones, took one of its boldest decisions. The central role of the Council in the commissioning of books was replaced by a programme of block grants offered to the major publishers for them to publish a certain number of books under strict conditions. This was a substantial change, and the challenge was to devise new mechanisms to ensure sufficient variety and the maintenance of standards, and to support a reasonable balance across the whole spectrum of publishing. It is to the great credit of the Books Council and the publishers that the new regime proved an unqualified success acknowledged in 2009 by the Assembly Government awarding a sum of £300,000 for further development. In many ways, this was the fulfilment, in the form of a practical programme, of the vision the new director had outlined in her interview in *Llais Llyfrau* twenty-two years previously.[24]

Under the new arrangements, it was the publishers involved with children's books who bore the responsibility for producing leisure reading for children. The Council had already disbanded its Commissioning Panel for adults and had transferred the responsibility to the publishing houses. Applying the same principle to the sphere of children's books meant that there was no longer any need for a Children's Books Commissioning Panel, especially as ACCAC was by then responsible for commissioning far more reading material for children and schools.

One of the bodies with which the Books Council had co-operated during the Year of Reading was the Basic Skills Agency. By 2006, this collaboration secured a grant to create the new series of Welsh and English titles, *Stori Sydyn/Quick Reads*. Originally aimed at older readers with special needs, these short, enjoyable and topical books have proved popular with busy or reluctant readers, while children and Welsh learners also enjoy them.

The Assembly Government once again in 2008 looked to the Council to spearhead the Wales iteration of the UK-wide National Year of Reading. Responsibility for the campaign lay with the Education Division of the Welsh Government, and specific educational targets were set. The Council was charged with:

> Leading and co-ordinating a national campaign which would promote reading by devising events and activities centred on three themes –
> Gift a Book Week
> Communities Reading
> Establishing 50 Reading Clubs for boys in their early teens. [25]

By 2008, reading was considered one of the essential skills for employment in business or in new industries. The Council's reading campaigns showed that it was possible to reach out to reading communities that were traditionally considered inaccessible, and that books can create a bridge between fostering basic skills and moving on to more formal skills training. The impact of the year was thoroughly analysed within the Council itself, as well as by the government. In the opinion of external assessors appointed by the Education Division of the Welsh Government:

> The National Year of Reading in Wales was an innovative and effective programme of activities which succeeded in inspiring tens of thousands of people of all ages and backgrounds throughout Wales during 2008 . . . Equally important in terms of the long term advantages of the campaign is the fact that the Year of Reading in Wales was an opportunity to inaugurate pilot projects with the aim of promoting reading, and these provide important lessons which can form the basis of activities and programmes in the future.[26]

It is pleasing to note that the Gift a Book Week, the 2008 Reading Clubs, and the innovative new programme, Communities Reading, continued to receive funding from the Welsh Government, and, though the Basic Skills Agency has now been absorbed into government, the 'Stori Sydyn/Quick Reads' programme continues to flourish. To date, 52 Welsh titles and 50 English titles have appeared in the series.

In 2008, with an idea which placed a specifically Welsh spin on World Book Day, the pupils of Chwilog Primary School inspired schools throughout Wales to celebrate the birth date of T. Llew Jones. The Council co-ordinated Wales-wide activity on 9 October 2009, and since then, although the date has varied, Diwrnod Cofio T. Llew Jones has been held in schools annually, the centenary event in 2015 being of special significance. The transference of the Memorial Fund in 2019 means that Diwrnod Cofio T. Llew Jones now falls within the remit of the Council.

Elwyn Jones succeeded Gwerfyl Pierce Jones as director of the Books Council at the end of 2009. The inheritance of the National Year of Reading would be developed further. With the support of the Welsh Government, action was taken to further rationalise the Council's activities by combining the work of the committee which had been responsible for the arrangements for World

Book Day in Wales with that of the Children's Books Panel, thereby creating the Children's Books and Reading Promotional Panel. The original print edition of Catalog Llyfrau Plant (the children's book catalogue) has been superseded by a digital bilingual version made available on HWB, the WBC platform for schools.

As noted in other chapters, a new opportunity arose for the Council at the end of December 2012 when the Welsh Government granted a sum of £50,000 (which sadly would not be renewed) for the publication and marketing of English books from Wales which would attract children to reading for pleasure during their leisure time. In more recent times, the demise of Gomer Press' Pont imprint created a significant void, but Graffeg ventured into the field and have enjoyed much success since doing so, having produce 63 grant-supported paperbacks alone for children since August 2017. In 2014, the Welsh Government funded a WBC children's book initiative aimed at improving literacy levels and enhancing the volume and diversity of English language children's books in Wales. The two publishers chosen to take the scheme forward were Firefly Press, which focuses on works of fiction, and Atebol, who publish non-fiction material. Both publishers make their products available on various digital platforms. Firefly has published 66 grant-aided paperbacks for children since April 2014, and in spring 2021, for the second year running, was named Small Press of the Year (Wales) in the British Book Awards.

Reading remains an essential skill which must be mastered through practice, and the best practice occurs when immersed in the grip of a compelling story. Good stories are creative, leaving memorable presentations on the stage of a child's imagination. Additionally, in an age of false news, book publishers are required by law not to misinform their readers.

Highlights that remain in my memory, from the wealth of children's books produced during this era, include Margaret Jones's iconic illustrations for Gwyn Thomas's adaptation of the Mabinogi; Jenny Williams's vivid illustrations and her detailed depiction of country life in *Llyfr Hwiangerddi y Dref Wen*, and Jac Jones's inspired interpretation of Gwyn Thomas's poem, *Drama'r Nadolig*. Together with that picture of north Walian school-children caught reading Penri Jones' *Jabas* under the cover of their desks.

In our troubled world, there is even greater value in the loving embrace of a mother or father, a grandmother or grandfather, sharing a picture story book with a little child.

D. Geraint Lewis hails from Ynys-y-bwl, Pontypridd. His many roles have included County Librarian for Ceredigion, Deputy Director of Education for Ceredigion County Council, Chair of the Children's Literature Panel of the Arts Council of Wales and Chair of the Commissioning Panel (Children's Books) for the Welsh Books Council. His own book, *Geiriadur Gomer i'r Ifanc* (The Gomer Dictionary for Young People) won the Welsh-language nonfiction category of the Tir na-Nog awards in 1995.

Notes

[1] *Welsh in Education and Life: being the Report of the Departmental Committee appointed by the President of the Board of Education to inquire into the position of the Welsh Language and to advise as to its promotion in the Educational System of Wales* (London, HMSO, 1927).

[2] Ibid., p.149, par. 187.

[3] Alun R. Edwards, *Yr Hedyn Mwstard: Atgofion Alun R. Edwards* (Llandysul, Gwasg Gomer, 1980), p. 51.

[4] Ibid., pp. 53–4.

[5] R. E. Griffith, *Urdd Gobaith Cymru II 1946–1960* (Aberystwyth, Cwmni Urdd Gobaith Cymru, 1972), p. 181.

[6] Ibid.

[7] Ibid., pp. 26–7.

[8] *Report of the Committee on Welsh Language Publishing: Adroddiad y Pwyllgor Cyhoeddi Llyfrau Cymraeg* (London, HMSO, 1952).

[9] Ibid., p. 21, par. 25.

[10] Ibid., p. 21, par. 27.

[11] Rhiannon Jones, *Llyfrau Cymraeg i Blant: Rhestr gyflawn o'r llyfrau sydd mewn print, gyda nodiadau disgrifiadol* (Aberystwyth, Cyngor Llyfrau Cymraeg, 1975).

[12] Roger Boore, *Llyfrau Plant mewn Ieithoedd Lleiafrifol* (Caerdydd, Gwasg y Dref Wen, 1978), p. 7.

[13] Siân Teifi, *Cyfaredd y Cyfarwydd: astudiaeth o fywyd a gwaith y Prifardd T. Llew Jones* (Aberystwyth, Gwasg Cambria, 1982), p. 13.

[14] Mairwen Gwynn Jones, *Llenyddiaeth i Blant yng Nghymru* (Caerdydd, Cyngor Celfyddydau Cymru, 1974).

[15] Ibid., p. 2.

[16] Ibid., pp. 20–22.

[17] D. Geraint Lewis, 'Tir na n-Og Awards for Children's Books', *Llais Llyfrau/Book News* (Gaeaf / Winter 1988), 4–7.

[18] Cyngor yr Iaith Gymraeg, *Cyhoeddi yn yr Iaith Gymraeg / Council for the Welsh Language, Publishing in the Welsh Language* (London, HMSO, 1978).

[19] Ibid., p. 28, par. 82.

[20] Ibid, p. 28, par. 83.

[21] *Llyfrau Plant: Children's Books in Welsh 1900–1991* (Llyfrgell Genedlaethol Cymru, Cyngor Llyfrau Cymru, Adran Astudiaethau Gwybodaeth a Llyfrgellyddiaeth Prifysgol Cymru, Aberystwyth, [1997]).

[22] *Blwyddyn Darllen Genedlaethol 1998–99 Cymru: Adroddiad Diwedd Blwyddyn / National Year of Reading 1998–99 Wales: End of Year Report* (Cynulliad Cenedlaethol Cymru, Cyngor Llyfrau Cymru, 1999).

[23] 'Holi'r Cyfarwyddwr' in *Llais Llyfrau, autumn 1987, pp. 4–5.*

[24] D. Hywel E. Roberts, *Blwyddyn Darllen Genedlaethol 2008: Adroddiad mewnol a gomisiynwyd gan y Cyngor Llyfrau* (January 2009).

[25] *Gwerthusiad o'r Flwyddyn Darllen Genedlaethol yng Nghymru 2008* (Arad Consulting, 2009), p. 8, par. 32.

Fostering Reading for Pleasure

The *Survey of [Welsh-language] Books for Children and Young People* of 2017

Fostering Reading
for Pleasure

Siwan M. Rosser *on the* Survey of [Welsh-language]
Books for Children and Young People *of 2017*

Two centuries since the publication of the earliest books and magazines for children in Welsh, the book has become one of the essential objects of childhood. New parents are encouraged to share books with babies, not only to stimulate their linguistic awareness and give a boost to their communication skills, but also to reinforce the emotional bond between them. Losing oneself in a book is considered to open up children's imagination, allowing them to see and experience that which is beyond their immediate grasp. Book lovers have long understood this secret, of course, but now research is now proving the value of reading, and specifically of reading for pleasure, for mental health and wellbeing.[1]

However, despite the clear benefits of reading for pleasure, it is not easy to ensure that everyone can make the most of what it has to offer. Competition for children's attention limits their reading time, and the appeal of technology is difficult to resist. The constant pressure on school and library budgets means that the full range of current and vibrant Welsh-language publications is not easily and freely available to our young readers. Furthermore, Welsh-language books for children face additional pressure due to their minority context. These books do not only have to compete with technology, films and so on, but also with the colourful, vast and attractive English-language publishing industry. The result is that even those young Welsh speakers who are committed readers at, say, twelve years of age, achieve that mainly on the basis of reading in English.

Welsh-language books are part of their literary diet at school, and, perhaps, at home, but the books that are more likely to maintain their enthusiasm for reading are in English.

Still, there is little point complaining about Welsh children's bilingualism: it has been a meaningful and real part of their everyday lives for a century and more. In 1911, for example, E. Morgan Humphreys published his 'book for boys', *Dirgelwch yr Anialwch* (The Secret of the Desert), inspired by the fact that he had not been able to read such adventurous stories in Welsh.[2] When Mairwen Gwynn Jones examined the state of children's literature in Wales in 1974, she found that most primary and secondary school pupils from Cardiff, Aberystwyth and St. Asaph preferred to read English-language books to those in Welsh. The librarian at Ysgol Glan Clwyd stated at the time, 'Among the reasons for choosing English [books] was that there was much more choice and variety and that they were modern and up-to-date [...] Many feel that many current Welsh-language books are a pale shadow of English ones.'[3]

Fifty years later, the continuous efforts of authors, editors, publishers and the Books Council to lift Welsh-language books from the 'pale shadows' has transformed the publishing industry for children. But in the 2010s, with the impact of the economic recession threatening the Council's budget, the need arose to look afresh at its activities. In addition, the restructuring of its Reading Promotion and Children's Books Department had demonstrated the body's intention to redirect its work towards this area. Therefore, in 2016 I was commissioned by the Council to conduct a review of Welsh-language publications for children and young people.

This commission encouraged an evaluation of the factors shaping the publishing industry and proposed recommended reforms to enrich the reading experiences of young people in Welsh. As can be seen in D. Geraint Lewis's contribution above, over the past sixty years, the Books Council has laid the foundations to build a diverse and innovative books sector for children and young people in Welsh, and the aim of the review was to examine their sponsorship and promotion processes, in order to guide their strategic direction in this area. Specifically, the Council wanted to know if the number and range of publications, and the balance between original works and adaptations, was appropriate for each age group. In order to fulfil this requirement, the number of publications and their sales over the last decade were analysed, and a cross-section of those within the sector – including young readers, teachers, parents, librarians, authors, illustrators, booksellers and publishers – were consulted. I received an enthusiastic response from all corners, and I would like to sincerely thank everyone who made time for a chat, to send an email or complete a questionnaire.

The research led to a series of recommendations, with some of them, inevitably, going beyond the brief. After all, although the reading of a book is usually a solitary act, establishing and maintaining the habit of reading is a communal and cultural undertaking which depends on cooperation between the home, school, library and the wider cultural world. Creating a healthy cultural environment is essential to ensure a thriving publishing industry. Therefore, although the final report made recommendations to the Books Council, the implications are relevant to Welsh Government and every educational and cultural institution working with children and young adults. The aim of this chapter is to draw attention to some of the main findings, in the hope of initiating further discussion on as to how to foster a nation of lifelong readers.

The home is where the habit of reading is first nurtured but most children, particularly those who are not from Welsh-speaking families come into regular contact with Welsh-language books for the first time in the classroom. Schools have a key role, therefore, and it was heartening to see that 96% of the teachers who completed the online questionnaire believed that 'fostering reading for pleasure' was a priority. But only 58% believed that reading for pleasure was one of the priorities of the national curriculum, and 76% found it 'difficult to find enough time to foster reading for pleasure in the classroom'.[4]

Developing literacy skills is, of course central to the curriculum of every school but undoubtedly the teachers' comments reflect the impact of the literacy framework at that time, with its emphasis on 'read[ing] accurately', 'show[ing] an understanding of a variety of texts', 'recognis[ing] different layers of meaning' and 'expressing opinions'.[5] These are all necessary and laudable targets but they do not include any reference to imagination, creativity or reading for pleasure. In England, on the other hand, as well as equipping learners with strong linguistic skills, the aim of the national curriculum for English is to 'to develop their love of literature through widespread reading for enjoyment [and] ensure that all pupils [...] develop the habit of reading widely and often, for both pleasure and information [...and] appreciate our rich and varied literary heritage'.[6] 'Enjoyment and Choice' is a prominent principle in Scotland's literacy curriculum also, while fostering reading for pleasure is one of the growth targets in Ireland's national literacy strategy.[7]

Of course, the absence of terms such as 'pleasure' and 'enjoyment' has not prevented activities to promote reading for pleasure in Wales in recent times, but it has enabled such activities to be easily set aside given the other specific requirements for the literacy framework. However, since the publication of the *Survey of Books for Children and Young People* in 2017, there have been far-reaching changes in preparation and a new opportunity to embed the love of reading into the classroom. Graham Donaldson's report on education in Wales in 2015, *Successful Futures*, emphasised that teaching in the fields of languages, literacy and communication '...can generate a love of reading that will enrich lives and contribute to present and future well-being'.[8] In 2020, a new Curriculum for Wales was launched which states that the experience of literature 'fires the imagination', 'inspires creativity' and 'builds a lifelong love of literature', and that teachers should plan activities which '...should promote learners' interest in reading for enjoyment, for imaginative purposes and for learning'.[9] It is hoped therefore that this educational drive will help to enliven classroom practices, reform professional teacher training on reading for pleasure, and realise the recomendations of the review, namely that the Council should take a leading role in providing material for the educational sector and expand the service it offers to schools.

However, despite the essential role of the classroom in fostering readers, comments were received for the review which warned against tying the publishing industry for children too strictly to pedagogical strategies. The core belief of some of the contributors was that, in the words of one of them, we must 'spark the child's imagination, inspire enthusiasm and prove that reading is a medium of pleasure and satisfaction at the same time'.[10] Material with a strong educational flavour does not create readers: most are hooked by engaging, well-told stories and relevant and interesting non-fiction books. Such books can then be used imaginatively to enrich the curriculum and they can also be part of children's lives outside the classroom. Engaging books attract children and their parents to bookshops and libraries: those key safe spaces where children may discover books and become independent readers. Furthermore, this is material that can be promoted and adapted for broadcast and digital media. After all, such supplementary activities are not unimportant. Older readers expect to have access to virtual material which relates to their interests, and so should younger readers. The lack of Welsh-language literary voices in our digital streams was one of the reasons why a number of contributors aged 12 to 14 in the review felt that Welsh-language books were not relevant to their lives. The review therefore called on the Council to work with the creative industries in order to increase the support for Welsh-language books and build platforms to share literary and creative content which gives a central place to the voices of children and young people.

Turning to the range of publications funded under Council sponsorship, most contributors to the review were satisfied with the quality and variety of the books.[11] But many felt that too few genuinely successful books were being produced because the industry was not, in essence, adventurous enough. Attracting children and young people to read Welsh was felt that to be a difficult task, and several echoed the experiences of the contributors to Mairwen Gwynn Jones's report in the 1970s. One teacher, for example, stated 'After Year 2, definitely, children prefer to choose English-language books – often because they look more exciting.' In the opinion of another, there is 'a lack of variety of Welsh-language books which draw children to read. They read more consistently and more enthusiastically in English as there is more choice.'

Calls were made to create the conditions which would allow publishers, authors and illustrators to 'take risks' in order to respond to contemporary cultural trends and to produce ambitious high-quality material. Some, including booksellers, felt that there were more than enough books produced for the youngest children, and that these were so similar that they started to compete with each other.

The majority considered that the main gaps were for older children and young adults, with 75% believing that there were insufficient books for teenagers, and that more challenging and exacting material was required. Translation is one convenient and appropriate way of filling such gaps but it became clear that this was the most contentious issue of the review. Respondents to the questionnaire posted more comments on this topic than any other, revealing much passion and frustration. One stated: 'English-language novels can be read in the original. It is a waste of time and energy in my view to adapt them. Several of the translators are individuals who could be commissioned to write original works, together with other authors.' At the other end of the spectrum was this comment: 'Creating a good adaptation is a craft that should be recognised. I have had enough of the unfair criticism that adaptations are inferior to original works. Good, high-quality adaptations should be invested in.'

Although the majority saw the beneficial role of translation in ensuring provision and attracting readers, the general impression was that too many Welsh-language books for children and young adults were adaptations from English. It was felt that their famous authors and familiar covers overshadowed Welsh-language books and prevented the industry from investing in original works. From looking at the data regarding the Council's grant scheme, it was easy to see that these concerns reflected the reality of the situation. Over the previous decade, 70% of the books published each year were adaptations and every one of these (with the exception of series such as Tintin and Asterix) were translated from English. I felt that the balanced had tipped too much towards translating from English, and that it was necessary to foster a policy for adaptations that was more strategic and mindful in its choices. The review recommended in 2017 that the Books Council should not fund a greater number of translations than original books each year. In addition, strategic translation plans that include translation from other languages should be supported to include translating from other languages in order to enrich the provision, offer opportunities to read international works and to create diverse reading experiences. By 2019, the proportion of adaptations had dropped to 50% and the Council cooperated effectively with Wales Literature Exchange and others to expand the horizons of translation to languages beyond English. As a result, a guide for publishers, *Cyswllt Cyfieithu* (Translation Connect), was prepared to facilitate the adaptation of children's books from international languages.[12]

The Council was able to stimulate enterprise in the field of translation, and it was concluded that changes were needed in its financial structures in order to stimulate the production of more original works. Specifically, the review proposed that the Council should reform its grant regime to encourage publishers to apply for support which would give fairer renumeration to those authors and illustrators developing original works. But of course, in order to bring more original material to the market, more writers and illustrators had to be developed. Contributors to the review called for 'mentoring and development schemes for authors'. The comment 'What about searching for writing talent among ordinary people – parents, grandparents, teachers, sports instructors, mechanics [...] People who understand children!' came from one enthusiastic contributor. In reviewing the publications and the contributors' remarks, the enormous contribution to the world of children's and young people's literature made by our most prominent authors, such as Manon Steffan Ros and Gareth F. Williams became apparent. But it was also clear that the opportunities to develop new names were scarce. As a result, the review recommended that the Council collaborate more closely with external partners (including the publishers, Literature Wales, S4C, BBC Wales, the Urdd and the National Eisteddfod) to develop activities to foster ideas, mentor authors and encourage illustrators. Such cooperation was seen between the Council and Literature Wales, in providing residential courses at Tŷ Newydd (the National Writing Centre of Wales) to develop illustrated books, while the Urdd created new competitions to spark young talent.

In generating an innovative, creative field which depends on collaboration with authors of all ages and background, and from all parts of Wales (and beyond), the necessary conditions are also created for expanding and diversifying children's books. One of the main findings of the focus groups, held with children and young people, was a feeling that there was insufficient material relevant to their lives, and that the range and richness of Welsh-speakers' experiences was not sufficiently visible. Another strong element in their responses, which was confirmed by parents and teachers, was that Welsh-language books were seen as linguistically difficult. As a result, reading Welsh was not an easy or pleasant experience for many children and young people. In recommending that the Council fosters a publishing industry producing books that reflect a wider range of the experiences of young people in Wales from the point of view of their background, situation and characters, the review also concluded that further consideration was needed of the language and style of books, in order to make the reading experience more relevant and diverse for our young Welsh speakers.

Creating a relevant and contemporary culture of reading for pleasure is essential to fulfil the potential of the Curriculum for Wales; to meet the objective of the Wellbeing of Future Generations Act to create 'a Wales of vibrant culture and thriving Welsh language', and to reach the government's target of a million Welsh speakers by 2050. Furthermore, by ensuring that the books produced reflect and examine contemporary Wales's diversity, it contributes to building a more equal country. This is a principle which has grown in significance since the review's publication, with the impact of the Black Lives Matter movement intensifying the need to examine cultural practices around race, as well as gender, sexuality, disability and faith, in our children's books. For children of an ethnic minority background, for example, or children raised by gay parents, seeing themselves portrayed in books can rouse or reinforce their feeling of belonging to society. But as one contributor remarked: 'This can also help others (who are already represented) to learn more about their fellow citizens, and perhaps to be more ready to accept them, and to check their privilege. In order for Welsh to survive as a modern language, it is essential to recognise the diversity it has: the linguistic diversity, for sure, but also the diversity of those who speak it.'

We must invest significantly in order to stimulate creativity and produce diverse books, but the review also emphasised that coherent promotional activities need to be funded. Although the creation of new books should be encouraged, an additional conclusion was reached: that more attention needed to be given to those books already available, and to create more opportunity to hear about books and recommend them. Both Welsh speaking and non-Welsh speaking parents, for example, referred to their uncertainty around choosing which books to buy. Although those who were familiar with Welsh-language bookshops and magazines knew where to turn to for advice and news, there was a general feeling that it was not easy to discover information about children's books. Several recommendations were made to address this, and it is good to see their impact on activities such as the *Children's and Young Adults' Yearbook* and the increasing attention given to campaigns such as the Tir Na n-Og awards.

Undertaking this review was a very special experience which brought me into contact with a range of people who are enthusiastic about ensuring a creative and thriving future for Welsh-language books. Since completing it, several of those individuals have faced completely unprecedented challenges following the Covid-19 pandemic. The lockdown circumstances revealed how fragile the industry's economic situation is and how vital it is to secure long term financial support from Welsh Government for the publishing world and our libraries. But the significance of books also became more evident, as many appreciated them anew when faced with inactivity. Sales of Welsh-language books rose in general and there were fervent efforts to share video clips and ebooks for children in order to support the informal schools that emerged in homes up and down the country. Books about the pandemic were published in order to help children understand what was happening around them and the power of literature to provide comfort, entertainment and companionship at a time of uncertainty was valued. The world is changing and, as new challenges face us, there is as much need as ever for books for our children and young adults to help them on their journey.

Welsh-language literature for children and young adults is the main research area of **Siwan Rosser** in Cardiff University, where she is a senior lecturer in the School of Welsh, and its deputy Head. Her report, *Survey of* [Welsh-language] *Books for Children and Young People*, published in 2017, is now the template for the Council's strategy in this area.

Notes

1 For example, see P.M. Bal and M. Veltkamp, 'How does fiction reading influence empathy? An experimental investigation on the role of emotional transportation', *PLoS ONE*, 8:1 (2013). Available [Online] https://doi.org/10.1371/journal.pone.0055341.

2 See Bedwyr Lewis Jones, 'E.M. Humphreys' in Mairwen Gwynn Jones and Gwynn Jones, *Dewiniaid Difyr* (Llandysul: Gomer, 1983), p. 48.

3 Mairwen Gwynn Jones, *Llenyddiaeth i Blant yng Nghymru*, report to the Arts Council of Wales [unpublished], (1974), pp. 17–18.

4 Siwan M. Rosser, *Arolwg Llyfrau Plant a Phobl Ifanc* (Books Council of Wales), p. 28. Available [Online]: http://orca.cf.ac.uk/id/eprint/124029. English version https://llyfrau.cymru/wp-content/uploads/2021/01/Rosser_Report_-_Survey_of_Books_for_Children_and_Young_People_-_December_2017.pdf.

5 Welsh Government, *Cwricwlwm Cymru: Rhaglen Astudio ar gyfer Cymraeg, Cyfnodau Allweddol 2–4* (2015), p. 16. Available [Online]: https://hwb.gov.wales/cwricwlwm-cymru-2008/cyfnodau-allweddol-2-i-4/cymraeg-rhaglen-astudio-cyfnodau-allweddol-2-4/.

6 Department for Education, *The National Curriculum in England: Framework Document* (2014), p. 14. Available [Online]: https://www.gov.uk/government/publications/national-curriculum-in-england-framework-for-key-stages-1-to-4.

7 Education Scotland, *Curriculum for Excellence: Literacy Across Learning, Principles and Practice* (d.d.), p. 2. Available [Online]: https://education.gov.scot/Documents/literacy-across-learning-pp.pdf; Department of Education and Skills, *Literacy and Numeracy for Learning and Life: The National Strategy to Improve Literacy and Numeracy among Children and Young People 2011-2020* (2011), p. 17. Available [Online]: https://www.education.ie/en/publications/policy-reports/lit_num_strategy_full.pdf.

8 Graham Donaldson, *Successful Futures: An Independent Review of Curriculum and Assessment Arrangements in Wales* (2015), p. 48. Available [Online]: https://gov.wales/sites/default/files/publications/2018-03/successful-futures.pdf.

9 Welsh Government, *Curriculum for Wales Guidance* (2020), pp. 128, 161. Available [Online]: https://hwb.gov.wales/curriculum-for-wales.

10 All the direct quotations come from an unpublished database of comments received for the review during 2016–17.

11 Rosser, *Arolwg Llyfrau Plant a Phobl Ifanc*, p. 15.

12 Wales Literature Exchange, Literature Across Frontiers, Books Council of Wales, *Cyswllt Cyfieithu: Rhyngwladoli Profiadau Darllen Plant a Phobl Ifanc yn Gymraeg* (Books Council of Wales, 2020). Available [Online]: https://llyfrau.cymru/ein-polisiau/dogfennau-corfforaethol/ymchwil.

From Fax to Gwales.com

*How philosophy and systems
underpin an online hub for customer,
bookshop, librarian and publisher*

From Fax to Gwales.com

Phil Davies on how philosophy and systems underpin
an online hub for customer, bookshop, librarian and publisher

I joined the Books Council in 1987. At that time, it was Welsh children, organised by their schools, who were responsible for distributing its promotional materials, for example a books campaign catalogue. They would actually go from door to door, revisiting every house to collect orders for books, then calling a third time to deliver them. That had been the system even before the creation of the council, with those schools responsible for the highest sales receiving awards and trophies. The council's new publicity department, at that time, was still charged with organising an annual book festival in cooperation with the regional book societies, although the last one which I helped organise was the Ammanford Book Festival during my second year in office. Of course, by now, the last book societies have long since vanished, although these were responsible for creating the council in the first place, and indeed they continued to be represented on the executive committee of the council for decades.

The council's trade periodical, *Llais Llyfrau / Book News Wales*, appeared regularly with articles, reviews and news of the book world, and a series of excellent editors made it a forum for authors and scholars to discuss matters relevant to the world of publishing. The council's children's books department did not exist in 1987, although the National Centre for Children's Literature had by then already relocated to Castell Brychan, with responsibility for the children's books collection, the Tir na n-Og prize and the annual conference, among other initiatives. The children's book club, Clwb Sbondonics, had been founded, and the Sbondonics van was travelling the country; but there was no schools team or children's books catalogue, still less a World Book Day, let alone any of the activities, relating to the promotion of reading and literacy, with which we are familiar today.

When I was a research assistant at the College of Librarianship Wales in 1986, I came across a fax machine, which I was allowed to use by appointment at the Agricultural College next door. That miraculous technology reached Castell Brychan at the end of that decade. Bibliographic records for all new books coming into the Distribution Centre (then known as the Books Centre) were kept on record cards. Every month, these would be arranged in alphabetical order, typed up and sent to shops and libraries. Every quarter, three months' worth of these cards was organised in order of category, language and the alphabet, to produce a list of the season's books which would be included as an appendix in *Llais Llyfrau / Book News Wales*. Preparing the annual catalogue entailed a process of sifting and reorganising twelve months' worth of cards, and typing everything for a third time.

In that era, computer systems were fairly basic, and indeed such primitive machines were what the Distribution Centre and finance departments had to rely on, while other departments had to make do without. The world wide web would not be invented until 1989, the internet at the start of the 90s, while digital publications and ebooks lay on a far horizon! All the work of the council's editorial department was done on paper, with some authors' work even arriving as hand-written manuscripts. The design department's darkroom, meanwhile, was a cave of treasures, where bottles of cow gum and spray mount were in daily use.

At the distribution warehouse in Llanbadarn Fawr, daily distribution or online ordering were unimagined future services. Only two reps visited Welsh bookshops, collecting orders and writing them in order books, before posting them to the office, or calling in at the end of the day. Shops would phone or post their orders, then wait for the weekly delivery van to visit with the latest publications. One display van would attempt to call at all those primary schools that were members of Clwb Sbondonics. The Books Campaign was abandoned in 1989, releasing new resources to reach the public. An advertising supplement was created for distribution in community newspapers: Gwledd y Nadolig (Christmas Feast). Television advertising was tried for the first time, and an annual sale was inaugurated, the latter continuing until 2011. Jumping forward a little in time,

Llais Llyfrau / Books News Wales could not compete with more effective (and cost-effective) promotional initiatives, as, since the advent of the Gwales.com website in 1999, reviews had started being placed online.

In 1996, after a period of consultation and preparation lasting three years, and with grant aid secured from the National Lottery money, and later, European Llwybr-Pathway resources, a new computer system was purchased from Vista Computer Services (later known as Publishing Technology), to serve the whole council, including the Distribution Dentre. In terms of its application to the book trade, its main purpose was to organise stock and invoice booksellers. For the first time, it was possible to produce sophisticated reports and sales analyses, including lists of bestsellers, and sales statistics by rep, category, language and area. As part of this package, a database of book titles handled by the Distribution Centre was created, pooling all bibliographic information. And for the first time, all staff in the two buildings had access to that information, as computers were placed on almost every desk.

A bilingual version of the PubEasy online ordering module, which was used at the time by some of Britain's major publishers, was developed for the council. The original intention had been, in addition to developing the ordering system for booksellers, to allow libraries and schools access through a modem, enabling them to dial in and consult the new database. There was no thought of allowing public access. As plans progressed, however, the internet came into being, creating the opportunity to give public access to all information about books from Wales held on Books Council systems.

Thus, in 1999, Gwales.com came into being alongside Gwales/shop. For the first time ever, individuals from Waunfawr to Wagga Wagga could visit a website to find books from Wales. The site could be searched by language, category, title, author, publisher and ISBN. Children's books were listed by category and subject, as well as key stage and age range, while the inclusion of key words across all categories enhanced the search function, transforming staff's ability to find titles and appropriately advise customers – whether booksellers, librarians or schools – as well as facilitating the direct search online for books by individuals. Unfortunately, despite this huge investment into what one expert described as a 'Rolls Royce' system, the council could not take immediate advantage of all possible modules on it, because of a shortage of resources and staff. But as sales doubled and trebled over the years, it was realised that it was strong and flexible enough to cope with an increased workload, without further investment. The only exceptions were the adaptations needed for the approach of the year 2000 and the adoption of the 13-digit ISBN which were managed without any loss of service to customers.

By 2012, the fourth version of Gwales.com came into being, user experience improving each time the interface evolved, including the algorithm-driven display of titles on any individual's version of the Gwales home page. By March 2021, there were over 32,500 registered users (6,250 of them being new during 2020-21, despite the pandemic); most of them from Wales and England, but from 146 countries in total and 880 from the United States.

From the beginning, priority was given to servicing booksellers, reflecting a desire to see a substantial increase in orders. Several training visits were made to the main bookshops to show the merits of online ordering, and a portion of the new marketing money which came from Welsh Government to the grants department was earmarked for the purchase of computers and related equipment for bookshops. A total of 35 independent bookshops took advantage of this funding and an incentive scheme for shops was established which is extant today. A reduction is given to the main independent shops, based on their turnover through the Distribution Centre, although only a small number (16) continue to benefit today on the condition that they give priority to books in their stores and reach a target turnover. That same pot of money is now used to give the principal independent shops an additional discount, based on their turnover through the Distribution Centre. As the internet improved as a global customer experience, so did the process of searching and ordering, although many shops continued during this period to be frustrated by the speed of web connectivity in their area. For that reason, an offline version of Gwales/shop on CD-ROM was developed for the use of booksellers blighted by internet speed, or whose computer was competing with the fax and credit card machines on a slow phone line. A number of shops were anxious to have immediate access to information on prices and book availability, for example to inform preparations for sales at their own events.

Once shops had loaded the CD-ROM onto their own computer, they could update information online daily, or await the next copy in the post.

By developing an offline version of Gwales, we managed to take huge steps forward in another sphere, namely the collection and presentation of orders taken by sales reps. In the early days, Books Council school reps also had to work with a new adaptation to the Vista system, that allowed them to input direct electronic orders to the Distribution Centre. But a more complicated issue, driven by the council's inaugural remit to support bookshops (a philosophy or social policy as much as anything else) also affected the way in which the ordering system evolved in relation to schools. A practice was devised to encourage schools to have their orders supplied by a shop of their choice. As supplying schools was an important source of income for independent bookshops, the council had no wish to undermine this by supplying them directly. As a result, the online process put in place was one which respected the triangular arrangement of schools, shops and the Distribution Centre.

Another website which is part of the Gwales family, and which also respects this 'virtuous triangle', is Gwales/libraries. When Professor Hywel Roberts researched the needs of public libraries in Wales in 2005, he found that the principal source of information used by libraries was Gwales.com. He also discovered that the pattern of book ordering in Wales – especially for Welsh-language titles – was considerably more laborious than that for mainstream books through British wholesale suppliers. The recommendation was that a specific Gwales module should be created to meet the needs of this sector, and so work began on planning Gwales/libraries. Funding was obtained from CyMAL to pay the technical costs, and a panel of librarians offered advice on specific details. The intention was to create a website which could be used in libraries as a source of information to ease the book selection process. Thus libraries that wished to place their orders by electronic means could do so via the website at the same time. Although the order would be supplied by the Distribution Centre, the local bookshop of the library's choice would benefit financially. The website was launched in 2006, and although at one stage over half of Welsh public libraries used this arrangement to order Welsh-language and Welsh-interest books, by spring 2021 only five counties now use this method of ordering as developments in EDI have occurred.

As a result of these technological advances, 98% of all Distribution Centre orders arrive electronically (spring 2021), and a next-day service is given to booksellers all over Britain. Other such developments enabled the council to collect, process and analyse data, sales and bibliographical records in a much more efficient way across all its work centres, for internal, promotional, as well as external uses such as stakeholder communications. And, of course publishers, being the entities closest to the book – not least through their relationship with the author, their instigation of titles' marketing and promotional campaigns and their being the first to receive reviews and feature coverage – needed to be integrated into this centralised technological hub. Around 2005, an interface was created for publishers to input data to the Gwales bibliographical system and inform the council's information services department of details of forthcoming titles, and any changes made to a title's bibliographical data. This arrangement has transformed the effectiveness of both council and publishers in relation to a title's advent and development following publication. On the model of Nielsen Title Editor, publishers provide rich content for each book: author biographies, tables of contents, and long and enhanced descriptions of their books, as well as press releases, images and audio clips, short promotional films, book trailers and so on. By April 2021, a new interface was created which permits publishers to directly monitor their stock levels, sales, etc. Regular information, free of charge, is supplied to Nielsen, Bowker, BDS, Gardners and CLA (copyright licensing agency), with an ONIX download available for any bookshop to gain access also. As a result, libraries, educational institutions and booksellers throughout the world can find information about publications from Wales.

Another aspect to Gwales, which reflects the bilingual ethos of the council – situated as it is in a rural, Welsh-speaking area in which professional opportunities are scarce – is that the websites are fully bilingual. Gwales.com – which has become a flexible brand embracing the needs of libraries, schools, bookshops and publishers – as well as the council's own administrative practices, together have proven that Welsh is sufficiently flexible to cope with the most complex situations, and that it is possible to work and trade through the medium of Welsh without any disadvantage to the user. At the same time, care has been taken to ensure that information about all Welsh-language publications is available in English, so respecting the language choice of customers, booksellers, publishers and librarians alike.

In 2005, following the recommendations of the 'Joint Marketing Strategy' report, an information warehouse was created for the book trade; by today the website www.wbti.org.uk (Welsh Book Trade Info) is an essential resource which is regularly updated by external editors. It contains useful lists of publishers, booksellers, libraries, newspapers and periodicals, with an advice section on matters relevant to the publishing world, such as legal deposit, author contracts, the preparation of press releases, and information on ISBNs.

The council's response to the growth in the technology and market for epublishing was informed in part by two reports published in 2001: *Digitisation and Electronic Publishing: developing a strategy for book publishing in Wales* (Rightscom, November 2001), and *The Utilisation of ICT in the Marketing and Distribution of Welsh Books and Books of Welsh Interest* (Rightscom, September 2001). It is perhaps fair to conclude, in an historical context, that the council's approach to this field has been cautious, having only launched its own dedicated e-publishing platform for the industry, Ffolio.wales, in 2021. However, in studying the field and becoming apprised of developments in a global context, and remaining sensitive to its bilingual culture, the council understood from the outset that the industry here could not risk going down the wrong path. In the field of epublishing, the response of other countries where the native tongue is considered a minority language was similar to ours , namely to hold back in order to avoid getting fingers burnt. Unlike those countries, however, all our customers could use English and were eager to have the same experiences and choices through the medium of Welsh. In the end, the council had to show a lead and offer a way forward that was practical and affordable. The Language Technologies Unit of Canolfan Bedwyr at Bangor University was commissioned to prepare a background report on ebooks, and to draw up technical guidelines for publishers: *E-publishing in Welsh* (October 2011) and *E-publishing: Technical Guidelines for Publishers in Wales* (February 2012).

Following unfruitful collaborations and a funding application to establish an independent platform for hosting epublications, the council developed a relationship with Gardners, the largest wholesale book supplier in Britain. Gardners had already 'invented the wheel' as it were, and had invested considerable sums to create an administrative system both practical and secure. Funding was obtained from the Welsh government to complete the necessary work on the Gwales interface and a processing systems for secure payments, and so the council was able to offer the first ebooks to Gwales users in the spring of 2012. Cooperating with Gardners certainly enabled the council to offer ebooks in EPUB, PDF or MP3 formats to Gwales customers; but in theory it also allowed bookshops which had their own commercial websites to offer exactly the same books to their customers.

Unfortunately, however, the costs involved in adapting shop websites to cope with the change, and the annual fees for gaining access to Gardners data, meant that it was not practicable for more than a handful of independent shops to take advantage of this development. But one sector which definitely profited from this relationship with Gardners was libraries, as it was Askews – a Gardners subsidiary – which supplied ebooks to the Welsh libraries consortium. The whole industry, as well as the general reader, could clearly profit from the development.

In a more favourable economic climate, no doubt the council would have succeeded in creating an independent structure for producing and storing ebooks on behalf of Welsh authors and publishers. Nevertheless, by Christmas 2014 there were around 1,400 ebooks from Wales on sale on the Gwales website, almost 250 of them in Welsh. By 2021 that total had risen to 2,400 (including magazines), of which 900 were in Welsh. Ffolio now offers 1,000 ebooks (in both languages) direct to the public, and to other wholesalers, and booksellers receive a share in line with the Council's founding principle of working with shops.

The Welsh Government's Language Strategy identifies ebooks as an important area for development for the benefit of the Welsh language. Although there is no general agreement as to the eventual outcome of the growth of demand for electronic books, there is no denying the fact that a significant percentage of people enjoy reading books on electronic devices, which increases the demand for reading material from Wales in both languages – a demand it would be remiss to neglect. As well as offering ebooks through Gardners, the council also encourages publishers to come to an arrangement with Amazon to ensure that books are available on the Kindle device. Putting all the eggs in the Amazon basket would be unwise – especially in view of electronic developments happening daily – but it is reasonable to expect books from Wales to have a presence in the online bookstore which sold 80% of all ebooks during 2013-14 at the time that these policies were put in place.

Another change made to the Gwales website, in addition to developing the ability to sell ebooks, was to allow customers to choose a preferred bookshop. A detailed map showing the location of every shop was provided, and customers choosing to purchase directly were able to nominate a shop which would receive commission on the sale. A QR code was also provided which shops could display at the counter. By scanning the code, the customer gained access to the Gwales website, and the Castell Brychan system would recognise the shop and enable us to pay commission if the visit led to a sale. This was a return to one of the initial ambitions of Gwales, namely to channel orders through local bookshops. This was experimented with early on, turning eventually, following pressure from government, into a system of supplying individual orders directly. Present arrangements allow the council to offer a speedy and efficient distribution service to customers, while at the same time respecting the customer's wish to support high street shops. It was found during the Covid-19 lockdowns that this principle was one which the majority of customers valued. This proved that the foundational principle of supporting the market rather than competing with it was as sound as ever.

In the spring of 2013, public demand, and the response of politicians, led to a new phase of development, namely to create apps and support the adaptation of titles for their use. Pressure was growing to improve provision for users of iPads or tablets. The council's lead on this was supported by the government, in particular by Leighton Andrews, the minister then responsible for the Welsh language. It was decided to build on our existing investment in an app which had been created for *Golwg*. Yudu, the company which had developed Ap Golwg (a play on words conveying both 'app' and Welsh-language patronymics), created an affordable package where much of the work already done, and the terminology created, could be made use of. Ap Llyfrau Cymru and the Welsh Books App were launched at the National Eisteddfod that year. The original app was created for Apple devices (iPad, iPhone and iPad Touch), to be downloaded from the App Store; at that time only four books – three Welsh and one English – were available. This development was paid for by the grants department, and the target was reached thanks to the excellent support of a small number of publishers. Corresponding apps in Welsh and English were created so that users of either language could see and purchase the whole selection. By Christmas 2014, there were 25 titles in ap Llyfrau Cymru and the Welsh Books app, 17 of them in Welsh. In addition, the app was available at the time for Android devices, to be downloaded from Google Play. At the request of a number of magazine publishers, ap Cylchgronau Cymru and the Magazines of Wales app were created in 2014, but technological change meant a move away from apps as magazine publishers preferred to develop their own digital content online.

Who in 1987 would have been foolish enough to prophesy that the publishing world and the Books Council itself would be so radically transformed? It would perhaps be even more foolish to seek to predict the future, given the technological 'unknown unknowns' likely to appear in the next quarter of a century. One thing is certain: to stand still is to contract, while facing the future with confidence is the only way to benefit readers throughout Wales.

The crisis of Covid-19 has demonstrated that reading for pleasure and for information remains an essential part of life for many of us, whether it be the schoolchild lost in a fantasy novel, or a senior, discovering new worlds between two covers. Whether it be a pensioner finding company and community in her own language, or a teenager scrolling through a story on her phone and finding out that others share her feelings. This is the audience that must be served, in their chosen language, and it is the duty of the publishing industry to ensure that the chosen texts of readers are available on the technology they use.

Phil Davies spent thirty-five years in the book industry, twenty-seven of those as head of marketing at the Books Council.

In the Hands of Readers

Libraries and reader development

In the Hands of Readers

Bethan Hughes on libraries
and reader development

For anyone engaged in publishing, writing, selling and promoting books, the aim is to get books into the hands of readers to be read. As the poet Mererid Hopwood puts it:

> In the space between white and black lies the germ of all imagining.
>
> 'Dadeni' (Renaissance), 2001

That is to say, it is only when black print on the white page penetrates the mind, understanding and emotions of the reader that words and their meaning come alive. The children's writer, David Almond says something similar:

> A writer needs a reader if his writing is to live. I love black words on white paper. I spend hours, weeks, years getting words to work. I love to shape them and organise them. I love the way publishers bind them into books and make them appear to be perfect. The perfection is an illusion, of course. Every story is embryonic, unfinished. It only begins to achieve its full life when a reader turns the pages, when hard black print is transformed by the reader's imagination into voices and visions and dreams.
>
> *Books for Keeps* online, November 2007

There is no purpose to a publishing industry without a readership. Inspiring and attracting readers in both languages has been part of the work of the Books Council for years, and has developed more in recent times, often through co-operation with other organisations and sectors.

The relationship with libraries has been long-lasting and fruitful, with librarians as core members of the Council's committees and panels, so that we are able to share our experience of engaging with readers daily. We are there to advocate for the needs and interests of the reader, to bring the perspective of the ordinary reader (rather than the scholar or specialist) to discussions about strategies for promoting reading or distributing publishing grants. It was fervent pleading by a librarian on the Welsh-language Publishing Grants Panel that led to the idea of making funding available to authors to produce 'popular' fiction and biography. Along with the creation of creative editorial roles within publishing companies, this has contributed to what many have called a 'golden age' of fiction publishing over the last twenty years, the emergence of a generation of new authors and a substantial improvement in the standard and range of Welsh books in both languages.

The Tir na n-Og prizes for children's books in Welsh and English have from the outset been a partnership between the Council and the librarians' professional body, CILIP Cymru/Wales, to ensure financial support and the involvement of librarians on the judging panels. This has been a means, not only of profiting from the experience and knowledge of librarians in the sphere of children's books, but also of promoting the winning titles to young readers, families and schools through libraries.

Reader development is a term to define a proactive approach to bringing together readers and books, encouraging reader to reader engagement and focussing on the reading experience rather than on the perceived 'quality' of the books. The Estyn Allan training programme funded by the Arts Council of Wales (2002–05) developed the skills and knowledge of librarians in this area of work across the whole of Wales. The reader was placed at the centre of strategies for promoting the pleasure and enjoyment of reading for all ages. Literary discussion groups and book groups had been a place for discussing books and literature in Wales for decades, but the early 2000s saw a marked growth in the number of less formal reading groups, many hosted in libraries, others supported by libraries through the lending of sets of books. As partners, the Books Council supported those groups by organising events such as reader days and opportunities to promote reading through the media.

The promotion of reading in general, as opposed to promoting the sale of specific books, became increasingly central to the Council's work. Developments, especially in the field of encouraging children's reading, include the Bardd Plant Cymru/Children's Laureate Wales scheme jointly run with Literature Wales and S4C; the Darllen dros Gymru and Book Slam competitions for schools; the Llyfr Da/Fab Books author visits, and the establishment of Diwrnod T. Llew Jones Day to celebrate the work of one of our most distinguished children's writers. Darllen dros Gymru/Book Slam in particular, has been of the utmost importance in encouraging wider reading by children. Such reading in many ways was often outside young people's comfort zone and yet its key benefit was that the Slam introduced young readers to many new authors. The scheme has also been central to many schools' strategies in developing reading and interpretative skills.

One of the most successful promotional programmes in recent times has been the annual Summer Reading Challenge, run by public libraries and the Reading Agency. The Challenge encourages thousands of children to visit their local library to borrow and read books over the summer holidays. The emphasis is on reading for fun, in order to foster the habit of reading from choice, and it also maintains children's reading skills during the summer holidays. The Books Council has been a key partner in the delivery of the Challenge in Wales from the beginning, through securing bilingual resources for Wales and funding support for library activities.

There have been two National Years of Reading, with the Council taking the lead by establishing a multi-agency panel to direct strategy and an activities programme. Many of the partnerships created then still exist today. World Book Day has also become an important annual event in the Welsh book calendar. Activities and enthusiasm have been evident in schools, libraries and shops throughout the country. The Stori Sydyn/Quick Reads campaign commissions titles aimed to appeal to emergent and inexperienced adult readers.

The impact and benefits of reading on our emotional and mental wellbeing are increasingly being recognised. The concept of books on prescription (the therapeutic recommendation of specific books to help someone understand and deal with a range of conditions), originated in Wales, thanks to the work of Professor Neil Frude, in partnership with public libraries. Now branded and updated as Reading Well Books on Prescription, this bilingual scheme in Wales is offered at every public library in the country. The Books Council has played a pivotal role in delivering this programme, funded by Welsh Government to ensure that the recommended books, for adults and children, are available in Welsh for the first time.

With the growth and development of digital reading, the Council and public libraries have also worked closely to ensure readers in Wales have access to Welsh ebooks, navigating through the complexities of publishing and lending rights, to enable libraries to make ebooks for adults and children available to borrow. The Welsh-language and -interest ebooks available through Ffolio can now be supplied to Welsh libraries' providers of digital content platforms, ensuring that library users can access the latest content. Significantly, the Books Council helped to secure ebook lending rights to Welsh Reading Well titles, ensuring vital digital access to these titles during the pandemic, when library access was difficult for many.

Some might argue that it is the role of other agencies to promote reading, and that the proper business of the Books Council is to support the publishing industry. But by supporting a wide range of activities, and by developing living partnerships with schools, libraries, the media and others, the Council is also crucially developing the market for the industry. It shows leadership by encouraging creativity and by supporting new and innovative ideas and collaborations. One such example is working with Tŷ Newydd writing centre to pair up writers and illustrators to produce ideas for original Welsh picture books for children.

The Council also has access to government, and can argue the case for funding programmes and campaigns. When a child takes part in a competition, the books he or she reads will be long remembered, and books by the same authors will be noticed in a shop or a library. The reader who discusses a book in a reading group will discover new authors or a new genre and will venture to read unfamiliar works. Without readers, books have little purpose.

The task of attracting readers to books remains a challenge in the face of so much competition for the attention and time of both adults and children. But by its tireless work and co-operation, the Books Council of Wales has made a substantial, indeed priceless, contribution to the publishing industry and to the culture and life of the nation, keeping book publishing in Wales vibrant, as well as relevant.

With special thanks to Nia Gruffydd, Gwynedd Libraries Manager.

Bethan M. Hughes is Principal Librarian for Denbighshire County Council. As well as serving as a member of a range of Books Council of Wales panels for over thirty years, she has worked in close partnership with Council staff on initiatives such as the Summer Reading Challenge, Reading Well, and Tir na n-Og.

Hand-picked, Hand-delivered, Here to Stay

*How small independent bookshops
are for life, not just a pandemic*

Hand-picked,
Hand-delivered,
Here to Stay

Eirian James *shows how small independent bookshops*
are for life, not just a pandemic

When Palas Print opened in July 2002, I was acutely aware that the days when you put up your stall, opened the door, and expected people to come in, were long gone. We were taking over a business that had been in existence for eight years, and that business needed significant expansion to ensure a prosperous future for the shop and a living for me. We moved to larger premises in 2005, quickly doubling our turnover and further developing the business. Almost twenty years have passed since we first opened our doors, and we're still here, somewhat bruised and battered by various challenges – personal and professional, economic and cultural – that have come our way, but still thriving, innovating and championing good books.

My connection with the book industry began when I worked as a representative for the Books Council in the mid nineties. I learnt a lot about the way the industry worked, by means of regular visits to a wide range of shops, of very different character, throughout east and central Wales. This experience turned out to be of value in preparing the business plan for Palas Print, though the world and the book industry had changed a great deal by then. The web had become an important resource for collecting information; there was huge growth in selling online, and, at the same time, a decline in the numbers of readers of Welsh. In the late 2000s, we faced the challenge of the growth in ebooks, but by learning from the experience of the music industry, and by working together in our own industry, I think it has been possible for traditional book publishing and bookselling to thrive alongside the development of ebooks.

One of the most important things I learnt on my travels as a rep was how unique every town and shop was, and how every shop needs to reflect the community it is a part of. What works in Caernarfon does not of necessity work in Bala, Aberystwyth or Chepstow, and what is suitable for a small shop in a rural market town, where there is a high proportion of Welsh speakers, will not be right for a city like Swansea or Cardiff.

Something else I learnt, while setting up my business, is that across the country, you cannot make a living from selling nothing but Welsh-language and Wales-related books. You need other merchandise. What is available to customers varies from place to place and from shop to shop, depending on the taste and choices of the owner, and also on the community served. Almost every shop in Caernarfon is a Welsh-language shop, selling cards, CDs, gifts, crafts, art, pictures of Wales, and so on. And so, the other merchandise in Palas Print is books in English; 80 per cent of our stock is made up of books which reflect my own literary and general book interests (and those of my partner Sel and the staff), and which are also a reflection of the literature-loving community in this town.

This model appears to work well in Caernarfon – Welsh-language and Welsh-interest books presented side by side with English ones, and a market that appreciates talk and discussion about literature in both languages. But we must continue to develop, adapt and change the shop to keep loyal customers happy, to nurture new audiences, and to meet the needs of the next generation of readers growing up in the town. Over the past decades, I have observed an increasing pattern, both within Wales and beyond, of English-language bookshops selling merchandise other than books. This is a reflection of development in the industry as well as being, perhaps, a sign of the need to respond to new challenges. So it was not enough to open the door and expect customers to come flooding in. We needed to grow a customer base in the town, and hosting events in the shop and out in the community was a key part of developing the business.

I remember being extremely nervous about our first event – three books in English, and one of them an academic work. Would anybody come? I had sent postal invitations to friends (and anyone else I could think of), hoping they would come and support. I needn't have worried: the shop was packed that night. The authors were squeezed into the farthest corner, behind the Welsh books table, and I had to shout across the room (no PA!) in order to be heard. But, with the wine flowing and the talk unabated, and everyone enjoying themselves, we had our most successful day to date (in more than one respect!) Sales that day were three times higher than on any previous day. It was quite obvious that we needed to hold regular, popular and attractive events in Welsh and English... and we had to provide more professional staging.

I have lost count of the number of events we have ourselves hosted in the shop, in our garden, and elsewhere, often working in partnership with others. The latter have included Tŷ Newydd, Pontio, Galeri, PEN Cymru, local schools, libraries, Canolfan Noddfa community centre, and Disability Arts Wales. We have taken books and authors into schools and communities who wouldn't necessarily come to us naturally. We've opened up our garden as a playground and storytelling space, have taken activities – from beatboxing to cartooning – into former Communities First centres. We got the whole street (on which the shop is situated) involved in the Roald Dahl 100 centenary events marking the Welsh author's birth-date. We celebrate with local authors and performers when they publish work. We welcome authors, poets and performers from further afield. Close to our doorstep, they come from Cardiff and Caerffili, Oxford and London, Glasgow and Dublin. And they also come from as far afield as India, Africa, Cuba, Poland and Czechia. Such events are certainly hard work to organise, and not every one is equally successful.

That very first event of ours in 2002 included Charlotte Williams presenting her memoir *Sugar and Slate* (Planet), which won the Wales Book of the Year the following year, and is about to appear in a new edition from Parthian, after a shameful period of being out of print. One of the other titles promoted at that session was Katie Gramich and Catherine Brennan's *Welsh Women's Poetry, 1460–2001: An Anthology*. This was an academic title, quite literary and challenging. If I'm ever in any doubt about trying something different, I always think back to those early days, those events that challenged both ourselves and our audience.

While employed at the Books Council, I had worked at the bookshop at Hay Festival, and would dream of eventually being able to set up something similar to the festival itself, on my own patch. Years, later, in 2007, Gwŷl Arall (Another Festival), was set up by myself and three friends in just over five weeks. With a kitty of £80 we managed to organise twenty events attended by over 100 people in one weekend in July. It was a great success and the community urged us to carry on. Over the next twelve years, the festival has developed to host around 80 events over a weekend in July each year, while on three occasions, we took over Caernarfon Castle! Along the lines of Hay, but with a much more distinctly Welsh feel, the festival offers a huge variety of events and experiences, including literature, music, film, sport and walks, programmed in a way that encourages people to experiment with something new. I'm no longer involved with organising the event, but feel proud to have been able to pass it on to a younger, very capable team of organisers who are taking it to new places.

Like most people, before 2020, I had heard of neither Zoom nor Covid-19. Both have become an important part of daily life since then, and neither are going away any time soon. We organised our first Zoom event in April 2020, and throughout the pandemic we have regularly hosted events (independently or in partnership) for children and adults, in Welsh and in English. We have learnt along the way and are hopefully improving the digital experience for audience and performers, as social distancing restrictions continue to some degree. Nothing compares to a live event, in my opinion, but digital events certainly add another tool to the box, as far as audience engagement is concerned. They certainly offer the potential to increase accessibility in terms of presenting authors living far away from Caernarfon, as well as enhancing participation for the socially isolated, be they elderly people, carers, young parents or those with disabilities – either physical or neurological – who cannot travel, don't want to travel, or who simply find busy physical events overwhelming. We have been joined on Zoom by people just down the road, alongside others in Sheffield, Chicago, and even

Patagonia. This new situation has presented the opportunity to keep in touch with regulars and develop new relationships with customers and supporters worldwide. Once restrictions ease further, I will certainly go back to hosting live events (initially in our garden and eventually back in the shop itself), but we will also find a way of allowing new individuals to enjoy these events and to participate online.

Being an independent shop which doesn't directly depend on public funding means two things. It gives us freedom to be independent, adventurous and imaginative, and it also challenges us to develop our audience and to continue blazing a trail. As a member of the Booksellers Association, we have benefitted from schemes such as Independent Bookshop Week and Books Are My Bag. But it is certainly thanks to the Books Council that we indirectly benefit from the publishing grants which are the backbone of the industry in Wales, along with other schemes which they manage. These include marketing programmes and the schools service, while the Council's Outreach Scheme inspires us to host events which are important to our existence as a bookshop.

Schemes such as Festive [Christmas] Reads and Summer Reads, along with Novel of the Month, are also well established and important means to promote books and reading at a national level. And, following early consultation with shops, the Council showed leadership during the pandemic, putting into effect a training scheme for many shops to develop their social media skills and to support the instigation or development of shop websites, with a particular emphasis on selling online. Although Palas Print has had its own website since 2005, and its online sales facility since 2008 (with a direct link to our stock-control system), we had not actively promoted the site, since our preference was that customers visit the shop in person. But those foundations had been laid, and we found that we were ready, when the first lockdown hit, to make an overnight switch to an online-based sales model. We realised that our customers did already know of our website (but that most had simply previously chosen to visit in person, for a chat and browse). And so, when we were faced with the older part of our customer demographic having to shield at home, we were protected by the fact that so many of them moved swiftly to online ordering. It is the case that many other bookshops were forced to cease trading altogether during these early weeks of lockdown, when the Distribution Centre of the Books Council itself had to close. But for ourselves, our service was able to continue through our website, email and social media, as well as good old telephone sales. And we found a way to deliver goods safely to those for whom books are essential, including an exponentially increased number of parents ordering books online to help them home-school, as well as customers making the best of lockdown to catch up with their reading or, indeed, to start learning Welsh. Our experience proves that small independent shops are appreciated by customers as an essential part of the economy, even during a pandemic.

What, then are the challenges for the future? The development in new forms of digital reading is still a threat to bookshops. Ebooks and ereading are certainly here to stay, and yet surveys show that children, in particular,[1] still value traditional print books over electronic book-reading while young people under twenty-four are of a similar opinion.[2] The effect of smartphones, in particular, is perhaps more of a threat than ereaders to paid journalism and the readership for magazines rather than books, and we do not yet know how the attention span of young people will impact on their ability to sit down with a multi-layered novel or well-argued nonfiction title.

All bookshops face many challenges, and yet, following years of decline, the number of independent bookshops is gradually growing again, including during the pandemic, while several Welsh shops have changed hands or opened their doors for the first time, offering a livelihood for a new generation of booksellers with new and innovative ideas and approaches.

We have recently seen that there are fewer speakers and readers of Welsh, which sets the publishing world and booksellers a challenge to reach the maximum possible audience for every book, not only when a book is launched, but in the medium and long term. One of our most successful and popular regular community events is Panad a Sgwrs (a cuppa and a chat), established for people, learning or wanting to improve their Welsh, who want to get together with locals and talk informally over a cuppa. It is a joy to see each learner developing their new skill, and gradually moving, from asking for 'a panad' in Welsh, to using the language with sophistication, to having a conversation about politics, the environment, or just books. The target set by the Welsh Government, to create 1 million Welsh Speakers by 2050, has certainly focused the mind of those running many institutions and organisations on teaching Welsh. Though my customers live in the town with the highest percentage of Welsh speakers anywhere in the world, even we have seen a huge increase over the past few years in interest in the language, in improving Welsh-language skills and in actually learning how to speak and read it. The pandemic has, of course, meant that Paned a Sgwrs cannot happen in the shop; however, it continues online, and we will soon reconvene in the garden. This period has also seen a huge increase in the number of Welsh learners, and a corresponding increase in sales of materials for learners.

The media seem obsessed with the decline of the high street and the promotion of Amazon, to the point of making it happen. There are certainly things that should happen at the level of Welsh Government to support the high street, as well as the bookshops that hope to continue trading on them. One would be a wholescale review of the system for business rates and rents and its relationship to local rates, and to consider revising it to plug the leakage of resources towards big businesses which don't pay their fair share of local rates nor rents, and yet benefit.

But still the past year has shown, even more clearly than ever, that the eulogy for the high street is premature. Booksellers (and other independent, local shops) everywhere have risen to the challenge of ensuring a steady supply of high-quality goods, with personalised service and local, sustainable delivery routes that reach anyone and everyone needing comfort, solace, or practical help to get them through the pandemic – and beyond.

I have described above the many activities that we have undertaken, and often instigated ourselves at Palas Print. But we are one small cog in a huge and complex industry, part of a network of brilliant bookshops across Wales and beyond, bringing books and readers together. Each and every one of those shops does their own thing, doing it with passion, commitment, and often with very little resources. Each shop has its own story to tell, its own special identity, as part of a wider community of independent shops and small and large towns across the country. Support them, and they will look after you and your community, offering great customer service, choice, and diversity, and a passion for books, reading and love of literature.

Eirian James runs Palas Print bookshop in Caernarfon.

Notes

[1] Book Trust/Open University survey quoted in *The Bookseller*, Natasha Onwuemezi, 'Survey finds 76% of children prefer print books', 11 February, 2016 (accessed 10 May, 2021).

[2] Voxburner/Bookseller survey quoted in *The Bookseller*, Charlotte Eyre, 'Nearly three quarters of young people prefer print', 25 September, 2014 (accessed 10 May, 2021).

The Creative Partnership

The author and the editor

The Creative Partnership

Alun Jones on the author and the editor

One of the significant developments in the world of Welsh publishing in the past twenty years has been the investment in creative editing. This followed on from the Books Council's initial success in securing commissioning money that for the first time allowed publishers to commission work from authors and so respond directly to market needs. Before then, publishers had depended upon receiving unsolicited manuscripts. But once a grant for commissioning became available, it was a natural next step to develop a new system that enabled author and editor to co-operate in producing work of marketable quality. I was privileged to be part of those developments, working on the basis of my experience in the world of education.

As a teacher of Welsh, I was deeply conscious that a high proportion of pupils had to struggle to ensure correct spellings and mutations, along with correct syntax; things that came easily only to a naturally gifted few. But what then could I do to stretch those better pupils who needed little routine remedial support? When I asked for a poem or short story it was not often that we rested content with their first draft; I would, rather, give them advice on how to develop it, and expect them to make the effort to write it again. We have long been fortunate in Wales to have the Urdd eisteddfodau to stimulate pupils by giving them the opportunity to compete in the literature section. And so generations of youngsters have come to appreciate that to develop their craft they would (at least, before the widespread use of computers) have to write two or three drafts of their work, at a time when the use of computers was not well established.

When I was invited to edit a series of volumes for young people – the

Pen Dafad series – I accepted on condition that we might encourage young authors, and in this connection I duly enjoyed happy co-operation with Nia Royles and Mared Roberts. At that time there was no guidance, course or training scheme available from the Books Council, so Nia and I followed our instincts as teachers of Welsh and asked of our budding authors the same questions that we put to our pupils. Does the opening of the novel grip the imagination of the reader and does the author hold our interest throughout the work? Are the characters properly developed? Does the dialogue flow, and has the author avoided the over-use of adjectives and images in the narrative? Are there too many coincidences and does the work have an effective ending? It was also necessary to consider whether the main characters were believable – believable while the novel was being read, not in cold blood after finishing it.

The establishing of the Pen Dafad series more or less coincided with the arrival of the digital age, and so our young authors had an advantage over the pupils I'd formerly taught. They now had computers, which make it easy to make changes and avoid the laborious work of rewriting or re-typing a whole story or novel. It is the computer which has made creative editing a practical possibility, to some degree. After editing the Pen Dafad series, I was invited to join Mared Roberts as an editor for Y Lolfa, and I therefore had to analyse what exactly the work of a creative editor entails. I realised that an editor must win the trust of a writer and co-operate successfully with every kind of author. I see it as teamwork, with both co-operating to create the finished product. I have been exceptionally fortunate to work with authors who have trusted me, and only once did I have to ask another editor to take my place because the partnership was not working. When a partnership is unsuccessful, that must be acknowledged.

There is room for an editor to discuss and argue with the author, but no editor should impose. It must be remembered that the author's name is the one that will appear on the book's cover and that she or he is the one who will take the credit and the strictures of reviewers alike. So it is the author's word that is final, and an editor must accept that and accept that one's role is only to make suggestions. Unnecessary changes should be avoided, and one should always be ready to explain and justify all proposals.

Naturally, authors vary enormously. Some novelists prefer to complete a work before sending it to an editor. Others prefer to send the opening part of a novel and ask for comments before sending the work a portion at a time. It is easy to draw attention to grammatical errors, but that is not the proper work of a creative editor. Obvious errors must of course be corrected, but it is for the proof-reader to ensure consistency and grammatical correctness.

The same principles which were applied to editing novels for young people can be applied to novels for adults. Perhaps certain aspects need more attention, such as: is the author too didactic, and is there scope for economy? Are the themes woven skilfully into the body of the work? It is a great responsibility to receive a novel and make suggestions as to how it might be developed. I must admit that I still feel nervous when I receive a new novel and face the challenge of making suggestions, usually about two pages of them. I do feel grateful when I see that the author has considered my suggestions, accepting some and rejecting others. That is how a team should co-operate.

It is very difficult to outline specific discussions which have taken place between me and individual writers, as the process is underpinned by a code of confidentiality between editor and author. I can nevertheless refer to a conference organised by the Books Council at which authors and editors got together for the first time, in my experience, some twenty years ago. I was quite new to the job, and so, rather than lecture, I decided to take the novelist Caryl Lewis with me to the conference, to discuss the process of editing the novel *Martha, Jac a Sianco*. As that was an open session, I can summarise here what was discussed.

Caryl begins the novel in a striking way by taking the three characters out into the fields in the dead of night to address the problem they've noticed that their cow is having with her teats: 'The three of them stared in silence at the cow... She sucked and sucked and she nibbled at it until the only thing connecting the teat to the udder was a thin strip of skin.' The implication of this, of course, was that the cow, by destroying her teats, had interrupted the circle of life. She would have no hope of rearing another calf because she would have no milk to feed it. As this scene occurred at the start of the story it was a strong and powerful symbol and a key image in the novel as a whole. As it happens, Caryl had created an additional chapter for the novel, one where there was hope of seeing new life on the hearth of Graig-ddu. She brought the son of Gwen the nurse to farm there: Jac had been her lover. There was much discussion about the suitability of including that chapter, and Caryl in the end concluded that it would be better to omit it lest it should interfere with the symbol of the cow without teats. Caryl deserves praise for her courage, as it is not easy for an author to jettison a whole chapter after making the effort to create it.

The discussion at the conference came as something of a shock to experienced authors, one of whom said, 'I wouldn't be happy to see a word changed, let alone a whole chapter.' But this was the start of a new era in the world of editing, one when editor and author have discussions, when an editor can challenge an author to reconsider aspects of the work. This is a dialogue that has continued and is still developing.

Creative editors are now accepted without question, especially by younger authors, who are eager to revise their work. I must admit that I have hesitated before suggesting to some people that the opening of a novel is not strong enough to hold the reader's interest, and that the work might be begun in a different way. I feel very pleased when an author responds positively by creating a completely new opening which far surpasses my own suggestions. And that is how it should be. The primary aim of any creative editor is to offer guidelines and suggest a new approach that may stimulate the writer to rethink. I thank all the authors with whom I've worked warmly for their patience and graciousness. I feel that by now many of them have become close friends; indeed, part of the family.

And I must also thank the Books Council for its support and guidance to editors. What has also given me great personal pleasure is to see younger authors (who have won Tir na n-Og prizes for books for young people) turning to adult fiction and producing substantial novels. That said, I don't wish to suggest that it is easier to write for young people than for adults. As Gareth F. Williams said on radio once, 'Young people respond to a novel with greater honesty, and they will say without fear or favour what their response is.' It is good to see Manon Steffan Ros, Haf Llewelyn, Lleucu Roberts and Caryl Lewis according the same respect and honour to novels for young people as they do to those intended for adult readers, just as did Gareth F. Williams when he was alive.

Every year the question is raised as to how much editing should there be of novels which have won the Daniel Owen Memorial Prize, and of winners of the Prose Medal at the National Eisteddfod. The question which should rather be asked is, which are more important, the judges of these competitions or the general reader. If it is the general reader, then editing may be essential for the author to be given the opportunity to revise, re-draft and perfect the work. Such is the nature of any creative process and the essence of the relationship between author and editor.

Alun Jones is one of the editors at Y Lolfa.

New Voices,
New Formats

The Parthian publishing house

New Voices,
New Formats

Richard Davies on the Parthian publishing house

It's a few years now since the Dylan Thomas centenary, but he'll be out of copyright in 2023. The centenary brought a wonderful surge of engagement with the writer's work and life and gave an insight into the powerful legacy he left from a relatively modest output. The centenary of the other Thomas (R.S.) passed quietly in 2013 while 2015 gave us a hundred years since the birth of Alun Lewis. These were all publishing opportunities in a culture of Welsh writing in English only now reaching some sort of maturity – in its earliest phases it centred on classic work from writers who at the time had to make the trek to London to seek their fortune. Posterity, so Dylan Thomas claimed, doesn't pay. Well, the history of his own reputation has proved that he got that one wrong.

Over the last twenty years Welsh writing in English has experienced a remarkable burst of creativity. There are now more writers than ever, working across a range of genres, and many of these are being published in Wales as the publishing industry itself has diversified and become more professional. Much of this has been due to the support of the Books Council of Wales, made possible in part by the Rosemary Butler report into Welsh culture in 2003 which provided a framework for Welsh government support for publishing in Wales. The result has been democracy in action, as a country began to take charge of its own literary culture in and through English.

The Butler report was the stimulus needed by the Books Council to frame a more professional approach to publishing – the commissioning of popular titles tied to sales targets, marketing support, again tied to sales targets, and a general emphasis on the improvement of standards in editing, design and sales, which has forced publishers to look carefully at their choices and their product. It also resulted in the creation of the Library of Wales series, after a recommendation to the then Assembly culture committee – by the writer and critic M. Wynn Thomas – for a series of classic reprints based on the successful Library of America model. Complementing the Butler report on planning for the future, was the decision of the then Arts Minister, Alun Pugh, to back some of its key recommendations and to ensure the investment needed. It was, in its way, an act of faith.

But then publishing always involves a leap of faith, a romance with the improbable, involving writers and readers and everything in between. There is something quixotic about publishing a book, so it's appropriate that the second book Parthian produced was titled *Tilting at Windmills* – a collection of stories chosen as winners of the Rhys Davies Award by Alun Richards in 1995. It was a slim volume, twelve stories from largely unknown writers who have largely stayed that way. However, it was a new venture – attractively produced and competitively priced – and containing new work from Welsh writers. To accompany it, there was a launch party in a Cardiff hotel, where Dai Smith spoke for the Rhys Davies Trust, and Alun Richards handed out the books. The initiative received a decent amount of press attention and soon, over two thousand copies of the book had been sold. It is a figure that may appear small, but while there are three million people in Wales, they do not all buy books – unfortunately. But what I think it demonstrated was that there was a market and an interest in Welsh writing in English beyond the familiar names of established writers and beyond a publishing industry controlled by London, resolutely uninterested in contemporary Welsh culture – although that was to change.

A quick history of publishing in English in Wales really starts with Cary Archard and Dannie Abse setting up Poetry Press Wales in the early 1980s, from which origins developed Seren Books. Before that, publishing seems to have been an ad hoc affair – carried out by companies such as Gomer in Llandysul, or Christopher Davies in Swansea bringing out the occasional title – with no coherent publishing programme or real attempt to reach beyond a narrow Welsh market, towards the wider world. The Welsh writers who were succeeding were published outside Wales, with Emyr Humphreys winning the Somerset Maugham Award, for instance, and Alun Richards publishing with Gollancz and Penguin. However, both these writers were reaching the latter part of their careers by the time publishing in Wales started to develop, even though Emyr Humphreys was still being referred to as a 'Young Welsh Writer in English', well into his sixties. In one essay reflecting on his journey as a writer, Humphreys considered the experience of arriving a generation too late onto a London literary scene in the fifties, when he was not, in his opinion, one of the angry young men who came to dominate the decade. Seren published *Shifts* by Christopher Meredith in 1988: the key book of a new generation of Welsh writing that was to emerge with the growth of Welsh publishing. More than twenty-five years after it was first published, it is still in print, and has moved into the realms of a modern classic – it is one of the books that has come to define one aspect of recent Welsh cultural history and to seem to occupy an emblematic place in the growth of publishing. And yet it still isn't available as an ebook, because the author doesn't believe in them. One of the challenges of publishing is meeting the expectations of an author as well as a reader.

An engagement with a wider world has been crucial to the development of a Welsh publishing industry. *Shifts* was reviewed in the *New York Times*, while Dai Smith, in his introduction and call to arms as editor of the Library of Wales, made it clear he wanted to create a series 'designed to ensure that all of the rich and extensive literature of Wales [...] will now be available to readers in and beyond Wales.' It is the 'beyond' that is crucial for Smith, as he has always seen our literature in English to be part of world literature, having himself studied at Oxford and then Columbia University before returning home. In his view, it is writers such as Alun Richards, Margiad Evans, Ron Berry and his old teacher, Gwyn Thomas, who have produced fiction good enough for a global audience, while remaining resolutely from and about Wales, 'a young country not afraid to remember what it might become'. The Library of Wales series, now encompassing fifty titles and sales of over 100,000 copies, confirms the nation's new engagement with its classic Welsh writing in English.

However, for a publisher, classics are not the same as new titles. It is new work that marks the romance of publishing and the saddling up of Rocinante. It seems only a few winters back that Parthian convinced the Cardiff Literary Festival to offer us a slot to launch our first book at Chapter and Verse Bookshop in the Morgan Arcade. The bookshop has gone – so has the literary festival – but the arcade is still there; so is Cardiff – and so are we. The book, *Work, Sex and Rugby*, has never been out of print and has been re-issued as a Parthian classic. If you stand around long enough…

It was the start of an adventure; publishing is fun, frustrating, anarchic, meritocratic, traditional, slow-moving, mercurial and dynamic. Publishing books enables you to meet the most interesting people: fanatics, storytellers, self-publicists, fakes, writers of literary genius. And to engage with words in all their variety and wonder; there is always another story worth telling, worth publishing, worth reading. I have now been publishing books for close to thirty years.

There is an element of celebration attached to publishing a book. It marks the end of a journey for a writer: years of work made physical between pages, bound, covered or appearing – as if by some black magic – backlit and moveable on an iPhone. For the writer, it is a time of hope and expectation: will the phone ring, the email or text arrive, the WhatsApp message, the Instagram post, the TikTok video, the tweet you can retweet to all those followers you don't really have? Yes, it's the publicist, Will you write an eight-hundred word blog on why you wrote this book of poetry/travel/memoir for a podcast? What's a podcast? It's a radio show digitally distributed. Are there any radio shows I can talk to? There's the *Review Show*. There's always a review show. How much will I get paid? It's for publicity purposes. Ah, I see. What about the *Sunday Times*? They haven't got back to us yet… And then the emails stop coming, the tweets fall silent, the profile dates and six months later a review of five lines appears in *New Poetry and Fiction with Some Memoirs* – online with a link to the new podcast And then it's onto the next book for both the writer and the publisher.

As I write this, I am conscious of the title provided – New voices, New Formats. As a publisher, we've invested heavily in ebooks but they are no longer a new format. Also not quite new are audiobooks, which seem to offer people with limited time a way to read books. I remember listening as a child to a recording of *The Railway Children* on a record player. I was confined to bed in a darkened room at the time with German measles, or maybe it was mumps. I can still remember the elation of the train, carrying the children's father home from prison, through the crackle of the recording; the excitement of the children and the call of my grandmother from the kitchen.

The real innovation for the future is always going to be in the writing. There's something already classic in a book – with pages well set, an attractive cover, something you can put in your pocket or carry onto a train and open, taking you into another world.

Richard Davies is the founder and publisher of Parthian.

'I Suddenly Felt Very Black and Very Welsh'

How the empathy that fiction teaches can be a tool for those who truly wish to create a more inclusive society

'I Suddenly Felt Very Black and Very Welsh'

***Lisa Sheppard** discusses how the empathy*
that fiction teaches can be a tool for those who truly wish
to create a more inclusive society

In their introduction to their pioneering work, *A Tolerant Nation?,* in 2003, Charlotte Williams, Paul O'Leary and Neil Evans note that fiction in Wales has been at the forefront of the process of redefining belonging, in the face of the country's changing cultural diversity. Those changes have been significant over the past quarter of a century. In 1997, the people of Wales voted for devolution by a tiny margin and, in 1999, the Assembly was established in Cardiff Bay. The process of devolution of power to Wales has continued since then, with a majority of the people of Wales voting in 2011 for greater powers for the Assembly, which became the Senedd, or Welsh Parliament, in 2020. During the same period, according to the most recent Census data available, there was a reduction in the number of Welsh speakers and in the number of those living in Wales who had been born in the country. At the same time, however, the number of people who defined themselves as 'Welsh' rose. The way we define belonging in Wales has seemingly changed.

Works of fiction published in the country, and about it, similarly reflects this latter trend. Welsh novels and short stories often deal with themes such as immigration, racism and multilingualism, and their authors come from increasingly diverse backgrounds as regards language, race and ethnicity. But what about 'how' we read, as well as 'what' we read? As Wales is a bilingual country, does the language in which we read have implications for inclusion? Are the stories we tell different in Welsh and English, and what impact does this fundamental duality have on our ability to imagine a fairer and more equal nation? By here discussing Welsh- and English-language fiction side by side, we can explore the possibility that Wales's linguistic divide has the potential to unite us as a nation, and make us think anew about how we define Welshness.

As it is just a reflection of the real world, or sometimes an escape from it, why is it important to discuss the role of fiction in promoting a more inclusive national identity? First of all, because it has the ability to convey a new aspect of our society, and to represent its different strands. In his renowned study of the development of nationalism, *Imagined Communities* (1983), the historian Benedict Anderson argued that the novel's development was central to the development of national identity – he considers the novel brings together groups of people who do not necessarily know each other, in the same way, it could be argued, that the nation unites various groups of people under a flag. It can be surmised, therefore, that the way that novels deal with characters from minorities or other groups on the margins of society can have an impact on the way they are accepted as part of the nation's society. In the United Kingdom as it is today, it is possible to argue that ethnic and racial minorities, and other groups on the margins, are still fighting for recognition.

In addition to acknowledging that some Welsh novelists had made a significant contribution to the process of reimagining society in Wales as a more multicultural one, Williams, O'Leary and Evans argue that the response of authors to multiculturalism is far more advanced than that of public figures such as politicians. Eighteen years later, reading the doubtful conclusions of the Westminster government's Commission on Race and Ethnic Disparities (published at the start of 2021), which claims that there is no institutional racism in the UK, it is difficult not to conclude that the understanding of politicians across Britain of the challenges facing minority communities has improved little since then. The difficulties of recent years have made it impossible to deny that racism and inequality are rooted in UK society. We were reminded of the racist foundations of many British institutions by the Black Lives Matter protests of the summer of

2020; accusations of racism were made against the royal family in its treatment of the Duchess of Sussex; the social and health disadvantages and inequalities of people of black or ethnic minority backgrounds were revealed by those groups being more likely to suffer from Covid-19 or die because of it; racism and xenophobia were part of the campaign to leave the European Union and the Westminster government's attempt to create a 'hostile environment' for immigrants, and the Windrush scandal, which led to those born in the Caribbean but living in the UK for decades being wrongly deported, is also fresh in the memory. It appears that many could benefit from reading more Welsh fiction!

But woe betide us if we think that these are UK, or England-only, problems, and that racism is a less serious issue here in Wales. It is sometimes tempting to think that Wales and the Welsh people have suffered racism of a kind, rather than manifesting it, due to the oppression they experienced following the conquest of Edward I, and later the 1536 Acts of Union, and the varying attempts since then to eradicate the Welsh language and its culture. Historians and cultural and literary critics have argued for decades now as to what extent Wales can be considered to be a postcolonial country in the same way as countries from all over the world who won their independence from powerful empires such as the British and French. The truth is, that although Welsh people have experienced (and continue to experience) prejudice and discrimination, they have also played a crucial role in the British Empire's efforts to oppress others across the globe. A number of contemporary authors in Wales have examined this, insisting that we need to face these uncomfortable facts if we are to imagine a more inclusive nation.

One of these is Charlotte Williams. As well as being a sociologist, she is the author of *Sugar and Slate* (Planet, 2002), an autobiographical novel which won the Wales Book of the Year prize in 2003. It tells the story of 'Charlotte Williams's experiences as a black Welsh woman raised in the Llandudno area of north Wales'. In addition, Charlotte's character's memories of her life mean that other parts of the novel focus on countries in north Africa, where she spent some time as a young child because of her father's work commitments, and Guyana in south America, where her father was born as a descendant of slaves and to where Charlotte moved to live with her husband for a period. In this way, *Sugar and*

Slate challenges the stereotypical ways of defining Welshness, in order to claim a place for black or mixed race people, such as Williams, in the history of Wales. A central element of the construction of the novel is the fact that she traces her travels between Africa, Guyana and Britain, thus mirroring the Atlantic slave trade, and reminding us of the role of Welsh people in that activity and in wider British colonialism. As Charlotte travels the world, she looks at how other cargoes completed corresponding journeys, centuries before, thus creating a dreadful connection between her story, the history of the black community and the history of industrial Wales:

> Perhaps the iron bar may have gone down in history as a simple fact of the industrial development of parts of Wales were it not for other world events [...] It was the ingenious coupling of iron hunger with a sudden increase in the need for labour on the West Indian sugar plantations that sealed a terrible fate. As the sugar industry grew in the Caribbean so did the need for manpower and this could only ever mean one thing – the evolution of a malignant trade. The African iron hunger was fed and strengthened by the trade in human beings [...] a great movement of human cargo to the Caribbean. Only by trading their fellow man could the Africans acquire the iron they needed so badly. Iron had become the back-bone of industrial development in many areas of Britain; in Wales in particular, the iron masters grew wealthier and wealthier, ploughing back the profits of spices and sugar and slaves to make more and more iron bars and then manacles, fetters, neck collars, chains, branding irons, thumb screws...

By emphasising the use made of Welsh iron in the international slave trade, Charlotte Williams links industrial Wales with Africa and the Caribbean, claiming a place in the nation's history for her black ancestors. More interestingly, the fact that she acknowledges that both the Welsh and the Africans themselves were responsible in a way for the beginning and continuation of this trade means that her story refuses to polarise simply between oppressors and the oppressed, reflecting Wales's own complex role in the history of Britain's colonial enterprises which we have not recognised fully, even today. In the novel, industrial Wales becomes a transitional space where Williams's Welsh, African and Caribbean heritage can coexist unexpectedly. This is clear in the title of her autobiographical novel, where the sugar of the Caribbean plantations combines with the slate mined in north Wales since Roman times.

Williams's novel compels us to recognise the presence of black people and black communities in Wales, today and yesterday. There is a tendency on occasion, by people in Wales and beyond, to disregard the black and ethnic communities who live here, or ignore them completely, because they are comparatively small in number in many parts of the country, particularly outside cities such as Cardiff, Swansea and Newport. The attention given by Charlotte Williams to north Wales is particularly important in this respect – in telling the story of her upbringing in the Llandudno area, she challenges the stereotype of Wales which portrays the south as an urban, industrial and multicultural area, and the north as a rural, isolated and shut-off one. The harmful effect of this stereotype is to be seen as Charlotte describes herself in terms of what she calls 'not-identities' – reminding her of '[growing] up in a small Welsh town amongst people with pale faces, feeling that to be half Welsh and half Afro-Caribbean was always to be half of something but never quite anything whole at all.' This is shown in her conversation with her friend Suzanne from Cardiff, where they both talk about their relationship with Wales:

> I thought Suzanne was lucky. She's Cardiff black and that's at least a recognised, albeit tiny, patch of Wales shaded with a little colour...
> 'You're not so bothered about the roots business Suzanne, because you've got roots,' I said. 'Africans have been in Cardiff for a hundred and fifty years at least. You don't need to go checking out your ancestors, they're right there on your doorstep explaining you... You're Welsh all right. I envy you that,' I said.
> 'You've got that one wrong for a start. I belong to a little bit of Cardiff, not Wales at all. Wales, what's that?' she asked.

Here it is not only Charlotte who feels that she does not belong to Wales because of the colour of her skin. The black community of Butetown, the community to which Suzanne belongs, feels that any sense of belonging is confined to one small part of Wales, rather than the whole country. They do not feel they belong to the whole country because of the stereotype that multiculturalism in Wales is to be found in the cities in the south only, and in Cardiff, in particular, and the tendency to neglect or ignore multiculturalism as a reality that the whole of Wales must accept.

Angharad Price's novel, *Caersaint* (2010), also challenges this stereotype, as it follows the ups and downs of a multicultural Welsh-speaking community in north Wales. Caersaint is the name that Price gives to the semi-imagined Caernarfon that the novel depicts, and the town's characters reject the idea of centralising political and cultural power in Cardiff. This is what is portrayed in the election which is at the hub of the novel. Caersaint is about to elect a mayor, and the residents must choose between two candidates: Medwyn Parri, a corrupt businessman, and Jamal Gwyn Jones, who allows the public to draw up his manifesto, promising to give them a voice if he wins. In an interview discussing the novel at the time of its publication, Angharad Price stated that she shared her characters' dissatisfaction with the tendency to centralise institutions in Cardiff, and that this was connected to her wish to challenge stereotypical and essentialised ideas about the nature of Welsh-speaking Wales:

> It gets on my nerves sometimes, hearing people talk about the north, or the west, like some kind of old fashioned, introverted Welsh places with some obsession with cultural purity and so on. That's not true at all. Caernarfon, for example, has been a cosmopolitan place for centuries – long before Cardiff!

The dialogue between Caersaint and Cardiff in the novel is a way of challenging the idea that south Wales, and the capital city especially, is the location of multicultural Wales, and that areas such as north Wales stick to a cultural uniformity.

The novel tackles this tension by examining what is meant by 'purity', in relationship to language, race and culture; and in the end, it undermines the validity of the concept. The main protagonist of 'purity' in the novel is the late Arfonia Bugbird, who had 'spent her life trying to be pure'. Despite her obsession, after her death, it is revealed that she left her house to a 'half saint [the novel's term for a resident of the town], half blood and half Muslim. A coffee-coloured lad from Saron Bach, via a Caersaint care home', namely Jamal Gwyn Jones, the son of a local, white Welsh woman and a Pakistani man, who tries unsuccessfully to be elected mayor of Caersaint. The concept of purity is linked here with race and ethnicity, therefore, and this is echoed several times by the novel's references to cleaning. In a conversation between Jamal and his neighbours, Trefor and Miriam, Trefor questions Jamal about the colour of his skin before expanding on his own mixed ethnic background:

> 'You're OK as well, considering. OK-brown, I mean. You could pass as a saint in need of scrubbing up [...] To tell the truth, you are not much browner than Miriam [...] Her family were Gypsies. Those Roma. Not the Segontium Romans, she is not as old as that. The others...'
> [...]
> 'Mam used to call me Gwyn [the name means white],' [Jamal said] after, arguing with him [...]
> 'Gwyn? And you being half-caste? That's the best, that is!'
> [...] A gasp of disappointment came from Miriam [...]
> 'Hey, hold on, I am not being racist, if that is what you're thinking,' [Trefor said] [...] 'my granddad was a Paddy. And Gran herself had Spanish blood, same as most people from the Llŷn.'

Although he denies being racist, Trefor's words are extremely insulting and discriminatory towards people on the basis of their ethnic background. But the fact that Trefor questions Jamal's mother's decision to call him 'Gwyn' creates doubt about the stability of the 'white' ethnic group. The mixed ethnic backgrounds of Miriam and Trefor themselves suggest that there is no such ethnic purity as that represented by the word 'white'. The name 'Gwyn' complicates Jamal's indentity, suggesting that identity is much more slippery and subjective than that expressed by hard and fast categories such as white/black. This is reflected in the irony of the conversation where Trefor's racism reveals his own mixed ethnic background in due course.

Jamal's slippery identity and name is an important part of his campaign to become mayor, and in the novel's attempt to make us recognise the history of racism and prejudice that underpins our everyday lives. Jamal does not have a firm name – he is described in the local newspaper as 'Jamal Gwyn Jones, aka, Jaman Jones, aka Jaman Gwyn, aka Gwyn Jones'. The playfulness of his name is suggestive, as well as being central to his political campaign, which is managed by Babs Ink, a local journalist. It is she who insists that he calls himself 'Jaman Gwyn' for the election. 'Jaman' was Jamal's nickname at school and it has both positive and negative connotations for the novel's portrayal of a multicultural community. 'Jaman' is the dialect word for 'bad luck' in Caersaint, which connects his Pakistani ethnicity (shown by the name 'Jamal') with negativity – similar to Trefor's description of him as 'OK-brown'. But the fact that he has a nickname to begin with shows that he belongs to the community – everyone in Caersaint has a nickname. The act of changing his name is suggestive in the colonial context also, as it reminds us of the way that Welsh surnames and place names were changed following the English conquest, as well as the way that representatives of the British Empire (including Welsh people) gave new names to slaves and other colonial inhabitants across the world. Jamal's name therefore represents the cultural variety of Wales today, as well as the history of its ambiguous relationship with oppressed countries around the globe.

Another novel which explores how slippery is our understanding of identity is *The Hiding Place* (2000) by Trezza Azzopardi, which reached the Booker Prize shortlist in 2000, and which follows the life of Dolores Gauci, the youngest of six girls born in Tiger Bay to Frankie, an immigrant from Malta, and Mary, a Welsh woman from Dowlais. Following the death of her mother, Dolores comes back to Tiger Bay – or Cardiff Bay, as it is now known – after living for years in Nottingham, and memories come flooding back of her childhood in the 1960s. One of these is the conversations she had with her sister Francesca about the boyfriend she had in the children's home where she lived. Francesca insists 'don't tell Mamma [...] She wouldn't like it [...] He's a Half-Caste'. This instruction confuses Dolores and she muses on it at night:

> I lie awake waiting for my mother to come up. I can't sleep until I've asked her about half-caste. Because that's what *we* are: that's what they call us at school. I can't see why my mother wouldn't like Fran's boyfriend if he's just the same as us.

Dolores and her sisters are not mixed race; they are white, but they suffer similar prejudice as the children of immigrants. We see here, therefore, as in *Caersaint*, that identity, and the 'white' category in particular, is a changing thing. Compared to Fran's boyfriend who is mixed race, the girls are considered white; but in the view of their peers (white, Welsh, I imagine) at school, it is easier to exclude them on the basis of their identity as second-generation immigrants. But in addition to that, Fran has internalised what the community believes, as she herself calls her boyfriend 'Half-Caste'. Although the girls are somewhat excluded from society and suffer its prejudices, they are also part of society in that they reinforce its language and racism. They both suffer and exercise oppression.

The Gauci sisters live between two worlds, but never feel at home in either. In his acclaimed essay, *Reflections on Exile*, the scholar Edward W. Said noted that knowledge of two worlds existing side by side was a characteristic of the world view of the exile – the world that they had left, and the one in which they now lived. In *The Hiding Place*, however, it is not only the characters who live between two worlds but also the multicultural community of Tiger Bay. The novel portrays the Gaucis' experience during two periods – the 1960s and at the turn of the millennium. Between these two periods, Tiger Bay experienced great change. In those parts of the novel which take place in the 1960s, additionally, we get detailed descriptions of the changes to the area. A number of the houses in Tiger Bay are being demolished, reflecting the exclusion of the family and the community to which a large number of its residents have migrated from other countries:

> [...] the houses on the dockside, near the saltings, are ancient back-to-backs. They have to be knocked down. Each week, another street is crushed to rubble; the grinding of the dumper-trucks gets louder, and overnight, a row of homes where people used to live becomes a stretch of broken brick and tangled wire. The sky gets wider every day.

The way that the sound of the houses' destruction gets louder and louder suggests how the family's fragile situation is worsening. As well as being literally homeless at times, there is not much that is homely or comfortable about the lives of the family and their relations. The description of the broken bricks reminds us that the family is falling apart – Frankie and Mary are quarrelling, one of their daughters, Marina, has had to go to Malta to live with her father's enemy after he lost her in a bet, and Frankie is trying to get rid of another daughter, Celesta, by arranging a marriage for her. Dolores herself is also 'broken', as it were, as she lost the fingers of her left hand in a house fire at a month old. On top of that, her father had hoped that Dolores would be a boy, as he had been cursed (in his opinion) with five daughters already.

When Dolores returns to Cardiff at the turn of the millennium, she sees that her childhood home has been completely changed once again, in order to create what is now called Cardiff Bay:

> This can't be right. The avenue is broad and new, shimmering with trees and pavement cafes. This is not where The Moonlight [a local eatery] should be: it should be in a side-street; narrow doors and fractured Windows [sic] and the cracked slab paving as grey as the Dowlais sky. This is not the place.

Despite the contrast between the 'side-street' and the new wide avenue, and the use of the word 'shimmering', which suggests a change for the better, it is clear that Dolores's awareness of both places – the old Tiger Bay and the new Cardiff Bay – makes her feel uncomfortable. The area's identity has experienced major changes, and it is significant that those affect Wales's largest multicultural communities. As a member of that community, Dolores feels foreign in this new location that has displaced her old home. Here we see another harmful effect of limiting Wales's multicultural community to a small corner of the country – with that area being almost entirely demolished to create a political and cultural centre for the new-look devolved nation and to build expensive flats, it is likely that that multicultural community would feel excluded from the area and the nation that the new development represented, as we see in Dolores's own reaction to Cardiff Bay. Although the novel was published twenty-one years ago, the scene is as timely now as then to the debate about multiculturalism in Wales, as one of the last remaining green spaces of the old Tiger Bay has been earmarked for the construction of a museum of military medicine, which would commemorate in part the same military forces which colonised the countries from which the ancestors of the multicultural community of Tiger Bay came. This misstep at best shows an ignorance of the history of the community of this area; at worst, it suggests complete indifference.

The novels of Charlotte Williams, Angharad Price and Trezza Azzopardi therefore not only reveal the existence of multicultural communities in different parts of Wales, they also portray the prejudice and racism that the members of these communities can face. Williams and Price, in particular, remind us of the history of activities by Welsh people on behalf of the British Empire. But they all also refer to the oppression and the subjugation that Welsh people themselves suffered, and this is reinforced by their wider discussion of the experiences of racial and ethnic minorities. Williams, for example, in describing her experience of attending an information session in order to prepare to go to Guyana to live with her husband, states, 'I suddenly felt very black and very Welsh,' when in the company of the other white, English ex-pats to be. In Azzopardi's work, it is not only the characters who are exiles, either – Wales is like an exile from its own terrority, at times. When Frankie reaches Wales for the first time, the immigration officer asks him disdainfully, 'First visit to Wales?' As Frankie answers, 'Yes, first time in England', the officer smiles and softens towards him, suggesting that perhaps he sees a similarity between Frankie's exile and his own experience of living in a country which is frequently ignored.

Wales in these titles incorporates the idea that is at the root of what the literary critic Kirsti Bohata discusses in her volume *Postcolonialism Revisited* (2004), namely that it is possible for societies to manifest as oppressors and the oppressed at the same time, in some circumstances. This is what is depicted in the novel *Gifted* (2007) by Nikita Lalwani, which reached the Man Booker Prize long list and the Costa First Novel Prize shortlist. The family of the main character, Rumika, hail from a family of Indian intellectuals, and Rumika herself is famed as a child for having an extraordinary talent for mathematics. Indeed, while Dolores's disability in *The Hiding Place* represents her broken life as a child of immigrants, it is Rumika's extraordinary talent, as well as her family's roots, which set her apart from her peers. In the first chapter, we hear that she cannot play in her friend's house as her mother does not like 'coloured people', and shortly after, her teacher says her talent makes her 'special. Different. Gifted.' Her ethnic difference and the difference her academic ability gives her are linked.

Education is one of the novel's main themes which highlights the tension between Indian and British identity. Continuous reference to education in the context of the relationship between Great Britain and India brings to mind one of the most famous documents of the British imperial age: the memorandum on Indian education in 1835 by the MP Thomas Babington Macaulay. He proposed changing the education system in India, in order to ensure 'the intellectual improvement of the people of [India]' and to make them 'thoroughly good English scholars'. The impact of Macaulay's attempt to impose British educational standards in India is to be seen in Rumika's story. At the beginning of the novel, her teacher, Mrs Gold, visits her parents to discuss with them the possibility that Rumika takes Mensa tests. The response of her father, Mahesh, reminds us that Indians are very used to being forced to conform to another country's educational standards:

> 'Have you heard of a place called Mensa?' said Mrs Gold.
> Mahesh felt exasperated. He had seen all the same adverts as her. The ads for this place she named with such careful tedium, as though she was rolling a diamond round her mouth. 'Mensa'. He'd seen their childish IQ tests, fooled around with filling them out in the Sunday papers. He knew what Mensa was, for goodness' sake. What did she take him for? And why was she so surprised that he and his daughter could string numbers together with reasonable panache? They were hardly shopkeepers.

Clearly, Mahesh has little time for the British ways of measuring an individual's abilities. The insulting way Mrs Gold explains to him what Mensa is, suggests that she sees him as someone beneath her. But Mahesh has a doctorate, and he is also guilty of regarding other people as below him, because he assumes that they do not possess his level of education. His statement at the end of the above quotation, that his family are not shopkeepers, for example, gives the impression that he looks down on those who are, and that he also has taken it upon himself to repeat the white people's stereotype of Asian people as corner-shop owners.

In this, Mahesh is almost representative of what Macaulay called 'a class of persons Indian in blood and colour, but English in tastes, in opinions, in morals and in intellect'. It is as if he has internalised a colonial way of thinking – he criticises those who have not succeeded academically, according to Western educational standards, in a similar way to how Mrs Gold treats him. He appears to reject the educational standards that Mrs Gold represents and yet he is determined to demonstrate that he achieves those standards. How much he venerates the British educational system is shown by him putting so much pressure on Rumika to attend Oxford University, a symbol of academic success of the highest quality in the United Kingdom and across the world.

In the case of Mahesh's attitudes towards education, it is not easy to tell the difference between oppressor and the oppressed in the novel. And when Mahesh tries to define his identity as a Hindu, the boundary between oppressor and oppressed becomes shaky again. In a conversation with his friend, the Scotsman, Whitefoot, Mahesh brings up the history of the partition of India in 1947, which led to the creation of modern Pakistan and India, and the violence that occured between Hindus and Muslims as a result. He describes his fellow Hindus as the recipients of Muslim violence, without considering that both sides had suffered and employed violence during the period. Whitefoot reminds him of the truth of the situation:

> 'I'm sorry to say this, man, but I want to know. Are you saying that you don't believe Hindus were massacring too? It was a civil war. You're an academic, you know the score – someone starts it and retribution runs the rest...'

It is interesting that it is a Scotsman that tries to remind Mahesh of the complex situation. It reminds us of the changeable roles of the United Kingdom's countries in the British Empire, as the Scots, similar to the Welsh, had colonised other countries over the world as well as suffering their own political and cultural oppression.

The fact that the family has moved to Wales reflects this duality. For large parts of the novel, no distinction is made between Wales and Britain. This is not necessarily caused by a lack of knowledge of the differences between the different countries in the United Kingdom. Perhaps it is a sign of the fact that Wales has played a role in the process of colonising India in the name of the British Empire. But there is a contrapuntal reading to be made here, one which suggests the awareness of two worlds which the exile possesses, as Edward Said has said.

Other experiences that took place in Wales at a different time are a backdrop to Rumika's family's experience of educational standards. Considering the fact that education as a weapon of colonialism is one of the novel's main themes, we are reminded of the report of the commissioners into the condition of education in Wales in 1847, which subjugated Wales to foreign educational standards in a similar way to India. The location of Rumika's family in Wales emphasises and reflects the duality that they possess, therefore, as it reminds us of the oppression suffered by Wales and India alike, and Wales's own double role in the colonial exploits of Britain and England.

Gifted reveals that it is sometimes difficult to determine who are the oppressors and who are the oppressed, in some situations of cultural tension. It shows also that it is difficult to define the relationship of different cultures to each other, in certain situations. That, perhaps, is characteristic of the experience of the people of Wales, when we consider the country's linguistic situation. In a bilingual country, what is the relationship between the two language communities, and which language possesses most cultural power? In Wales, Welsh speakers can claim a connection to a millennium and a half of Wales's history and literature, but at the same time they are a linguistic minority and continue to fight for rights and respect for their language, despite legislation in its favour. At the same time, English speakers represent the vast majority of the population of Wales, but feelings of inadequacy, regret or disadvantage haunt some, because they cannot speak Welsh. It begs the question, which culture is Wales's 'main' culture – the Welsh-language culture that can be dated back to the early Middle Ages and which continues in some form today, or the English-language culture which the majority of the population professes? This is an important issue for any debate on multiculturalism in Wales, as is shown by the work of several academics, such as Charlotte Williams, Simon Brooks, Daniel G. Williams and Gwennan Higham, as it asks the question, with which culture should the nation's multicultural communities, or immigrants, try to relate?

As may be expected, this linguistic controversy is a constant theme in the work of several contemporary novelists, in both English and Welsh. One highly relevant novel is *Pan Oeddwn Fachgen* (When I Was a Boy) (2002) by Mihangel

Morgan. This is a fictional autobiography of an unnamed boy and the story of his upbringing in the valleys of south Wales in the 1960s. He is raised in a Welsh-speaking home in an area where the majority speak only English. At the start of the novel, there is what appears to be a note from the author saying: 'In this memoir, in my attempt to go back to the past, I have tried to resurrect the language as it was in my youth. Those who speak this dialect are rare today.' This is the Gwentian dialect, and the boy's use of it excludes him from his monolingual companions.

Another issue that alienates him from his peers is his transgender identity. As the narrative unfolds, the Welsh language is linked more and more with the boy's alternative gender. Both things are a constant source of teasing for the other local children. Arriving home from school one day, for example, a group of boys shout, 'Hey! Welshy!' at him and refuse to let him pass. Another time, the same boys drag him to the park and pull down his trousers, before shouting, 'Oh, he have got a bit of a cock after all,' suggesting that he has an effeminate manner. By setting these two incidents side by side on the same page, we get the impression that both aspects of his identity, his language and his gender, set him apart from everyone else.

But the note at the start of the novel also suggests that this text is more than an autobiography, that it is also some kind of linguistic study, an attempt to record and celebrate the characteristics of the Gwentian dialect and the Welsh-language culture of the south-east. Then, 'M.M.' tells us that the dialects of the south-east are his main interest and he could not 'resist the opportunity to try to resurrect the old community, the language as I remember it.' This aspect challenges the impression that the boy and his family are remarkable for speaking Welsh in an English-language area, as it reminds us that the area also has a wealth of Welsh-language traditions. The novel thereby demonstrates that it is not easy to define Wales's linguistic landscape as polarised between the Welsh and English languages. And the novel itself is even harder to define, if we consider the way it transforms genre towards the end. There, the character of Mr. Morris, the boy's friendly neighbour, takes up the reins of the narrative and admits to killing the boy and keeping the crime secret for many years, thus turning the novel into a kind of detective story as the reader tries to understand what has happened. Contemplating what he did, he says of the boy, 'his language was my language. His life was my life. And where there was a gap in his story, I filled it with my own story,' suggesting that he, rather than the boy, had been telling the story all along. This raises the question of who 'M.M.' is; whose signature is at the end of the note introducing the novel – is it Mihangel Morgan, or Mr. Morris? In a similar way to the way it delineates the area's linguistic identity, the nature of the novel itself is hard to conclusively determine.

The boy's transgender identity, together with Mr. Morris's alternative gender identity, reflects this also. At the end of the novel, he talks about his relationship with his wife Linda. It appears that their relationship is different because 'no one "wears the trousers", as they do say'. As well as referring to the traditional division of power in heterosexual relationships, this section suggests that the owner of this (Mr. Morris's) voice, as well as the young boy, cross-dresses or is transgender. There is a possibility, therefore, that Mr. Morris's voice is that of the boy, and that the act of killing him in the novel symbolises him accepting his complex gender identity. In this way, the gender politics of the novel examine that which literary critics internationally refer to in English as 'Queer'. Although the term's roots are as a word used pejoratively against gay people, what is of interest to literary critics in this field is to challenge the binary categories of masculinity and femininity, and heterosexuality and homosexuality, by contending that hard and fast dualities such as these do not reflect individuals' identities nor their experience of the world as it is.

If we also consider the treatment of the linguistic politics of Wales in *Pan Oeddwn Fachgen*, we see that it challenges the duality between the Welsh and English languages, as it is often used to divide different parts of Wales, and different communities of Welsh people, from each other. The attention the novel gives to the historical Welsh-language dialect of the south-eastern valleys disputes the supremacy of English in that area, a supremacy which alienates the boy from his peers in the same way as does his transgender identity.

In his autobiographical work, *Cyffesion Geordie Oddi Cartref* (The Confessions of a Geordie Away from Home) (2010), Tony Bianchi tackles the hierarchy around language in Wales, and in so doing, examines the modern nation and its historical and linguistic roots. He often uses his own story (as someone born in South Shields but who is fluent in Welsh) in his work to challenge stereotypes about language and belonging in Wales. In the story, 'Cyfraith, Trefn a Chrefft Sbenglyna' (Law, Order and the Art of the Strict Slam), for example, after he and his friend are called 'f***ing Welshy c**ts' by a drunk as they protest in Welsh on the streets of Cardiff, he shouts back 'I'm not a f***ing Welshy c**t… I'm a f***ing English c**t!', enjoying discomforting the drunk even more. Bianchi's character has what the cultural theorist Homi K. Bhabha calls 'the uncanny fluency of another's language', referring to the way that those migrants who master the languages of their new countries destabilise the apparently natural relationship between language and nationality. Bianchi's fluency in Welsh leads people to assume that he comes from Wales, but the fact that he challenges that assumption raises questions about the relationship between the Welsh language and Welshness.

In his story 'Neges o Frynaich' (A Message from Bernica), Bianchi destabilises the links between language, identity and territory even more thoroughly. Bianchi's character has been made a member of the Gorsedd (the association of Welsh bards) and has chosen 'Bryneichwr' (Bernican) as his bardic name, referring to his birth and upbringing in Northumberland, the county that now occupies the kingdom of Bernica, which was in existence during the time of the Britons and Anglo-Saxons. By choosing this name he is teasing his fellow bards, by boasting that his roots in the Old North (the 'Hen Ogledd' of early Welsh literature and history) give him a more genuine Welsh identity than theirs, arising as theirs does in the main from being born and raised in modern Wales. But soon his joke comes back to bite him as he receives an invitation from a woman by the name of Rhieinfellt to address the Goat's Heed Society outside Newcastle. The name of the society echoes the original name of Gateshead nearby, which emanated from the Latin 'Ad Caput Caprae', which in turn had its roots in an early Celtic name. This name, therefore, as well as the name 'Bryneichwr' emphasises that the territory of the Welsh language has changed over time. For Welsh speakers, it is famed as the region which spawned some of the earliest works of the literary tradition, such as *Y Gododdin*. But as it happens, it is also an important region in the history of English literature. It was home to the poet Caedmon, for example, the first English-language poet whose name we know.

And when Bianchi reaches Newcastle, a man who calls himself 'Caedmon' from the Goat's Heed Society takes him on a tour around his childhood home, reminding him of the area's English and English-language heritage. When Bianchi mistakes the red- and yellow- striped stickers he sees on car boots as the Catalonian flag, for example, Caedmon reminds him that it is the flag of St Oswald, the king of Northumbria which developed after Bernica and Deira united. The fact that he is being guided by a man named after the earliest English-language poet suggests that here is an attempt to become familiar with the English-language literary heritage of the area. Bianchi himself challenges notions about Welshness because he is an Englishman who speaks Welsh. In a similar manner, his journey to the Old North challenges our understanding of Welsh-language literary history, as it emphasises the presence of an English historical and an accompanying English-language literary narrative which co-exist with the Welsh, and emanate from the same place.

History in general and chronological time is disturbed in the story. The figure of Caedmon is ambiguous – is this the Anglo-Saxon poet himself, come from the past in order to help the character Bianchi reconnect with the history of Northumbria? Chronological time is disrupted, which makes it possible for Caedmon to cross the boundary between the present and past. This is reinforced by the way the story is framed, which sees Bianchi in Cardiff's old library, watching a young Muslim pray in the quiet of the Welsh-language books section.

It can be argued that this story belongs, in many ways, to the genre of magic realism. In attempting to define this genre, the literary critic Wendy B. Farris notes, 'these fictions disturb received ideas about time, space and identity'. This is the certainly the case for 'Neges o Frynaich', where the past and present flow into each other, where the territory of Bernica is considered both Welsh and English land and where identities, such as Bianchi's, challenge concepts of Welshness. Farris also suggests that, 'the closeness or near merging of two realms, two worlds, [is] another aspect of magical realism.' A number of worlds come together in this story: the figure of Caedmon connects the past and present;

the Bianchi character himself combines Welsh and English identities by assuming the name 'Bryneichwr', and the land of Bernica teems with the heritage of two countries and two languages. The characters and places in the story are ambiguous identities in themselves.

Ignoring the battles that had occured between the two sides, members of the Goat's Heed Society commemorate those times when their Welsh and English-speaking forefathers lived together peacefully. Caedmon emphasises also how both nations lived together side by side:

> There, out of view, he said, they lie – the Angles and the Welsh together, as they lived for a few years, under the same sun, on the same barren acres. Everyone lying in perfect peace, all curled up too, and that proves it, Caedmon said. Proves that they lived together, died together, were buried together. For a while, at least. And could speak both languages as well.

Then, the members of the Society perform a ritual, imitating their dead forefathers through lying on the floor in the crouched position and chanting:

> 'I am Gospadric,' said one to the heather. 'Alas my hand which struck my lord.'
>   'I am Gososwald,' said another to the stones. 'Alas my hand which struck my lord.'
>   'I am Goscubrycht,' said a third to the ground. 'Alas my hand which struck my lord.'
>   'In the midst of soil and my ancestors, alas my hand which struck my cousin,' said Caedmon.

Another secret about Caedmon is revealed here: he speaks Welsh. Caedmon, as a Welsh speaker and as an incarnation of an English-language poet, offers himself as a model for the Bianchi character to follow. This is suggested especially as Caedmon asks him to repeat the act of lying in the crouched [burial] position and commemorating these forefathers.

Bianchi keeps his promise and, at the end of the story, back in Cardiff's old library, he waits patiently for the young Muslim to finish his prayer, in order that he may perform his ritual. He lies down on the floor in that crouching position, reciting the words 'I am Bryneichwr [...] Alas my hand, the fate that befell me.'

The focus here on his 'hand' draws attention to his status as an author. Considering that Bryneichwr is a bardic name, perhaps the fate that he refers to is the fact that he was destined to be an author – after all, because of his upbringing in north-east England, he is heir to Welsh and English-language literary history. But the discomforting tone of his words suggest that the fate to which he refers is not one he welcomes. It could be argued that the Bianchi character feels that only as an author and through his writing can he combine his Welsh and English identities – through creating fictional, secret worlds such as Bernica here, where the boundaries between the past and present, fact and fiction, Welsh and English, and Wales and England fade. He can only belong to both Wales and England in a fictional world, because in the real world the divisions between who belongs, and who does not, are ever present, as the compulsion of the Muslim boy to pray among the Welsh-language books reveals.

It is interesting to consider that Bianchi's story suggests that it is among books, or in the literary world, rather than in the real world, that his multifaceted identity can thrive, thus echoing to a degree the remark by Williams, O'Leary and Evans, that fiction is at the cutting-edge in the process of creating a more inclusive society in Wales. It is also significant that the literary world that Bianchi delineates is a bilingual one, one which emphasises that which is common between the Welsh and English languages, rather than that which divides their speakers.

After all, this essay has also demonstrated that contemporary Welsh- and English-language fiction in Wales has much in common, particularly in the manner in which they discuss linguistic and cultural diversity. The literary critic M. Wynn Thomas, a pioneer in the field of literary studies in the way he has promoted comparative studies of Welsh and English-language literature, has remarked that it would be 'of interest to examine the possibility that Welsh-language literature and English-language literature in Wales have formed the vital "other" to each other in both directions, and that that "other" has influenced the development of both literatures.' That is to say, that the linguistic situation in Wales, which sees a continuing contention between Welsh and English as to which language is the 'main' language and which the 'other', actually drives our literary culture. It is almost impossible to understand the one, without understanding the other. Elsewhere, M. Wynn Thomas states his hope that promoting the reading of literature in both languages, side by side, would lead to 'the radical psychocultural restructuring of the country'.

Daring, therefore, to contribute to this restructuring, what if we were to take advantage of the continuous tussle between our two main languages, and rather than see it as a problem to be overcome, take the opportunity to challenge assumptions about the supremacy – and indeed, necessity – of one cultural 'mainstream' with which everyone must assimilate (a concept that dominates the British debate about identity and belonging)? By reading the fictional output of the twenty-first century in both Welsh and English, side-by-side, we can see that the fiction of both languages has, at the very least, much more in common than that which sets them apart. And as we read and understand the world through the eyes of each linguistic community, perhaps it will be possible to better imagine the experiences of different communities, and come to create a more inclusive and welcoming nation.

Of course, there are obstacles facing us in bringing off such a feat – not everyone can read Welsh and the English-language literary tradition in Wales has not historically had much attention. But we are, hopefully, on the threshold of change in the way we deal with language, literature and diversity as a nation, because of change to the education system. It is to be hoped that new practices in teaching Welsh as a second language will entail more numerous confident Welsh speakers. English-language literature from Wales has been part of the WJEC GCSE and A level modules for English Literature since 2014. And recently, following a report by Charlotte Williams into the way in which minority communities are represented in the classroom, the history of black and ethnic minority people in Wales has become an essential part of the curriculum. Although these changes raise other issues about the nature of Welshness, they also promote a more inclusive national identity. And as we foster new readers who are used to reading about Wales's cultural diversity in both languages, the hope is that our reading and writing community in Wales will also be more inclusive, and that we will all benefit from it.

Lisa Sheppard is a translator, author and researcher who deals with subjects such as multiculturalism, nationality and gender. She is the author of *Y Gymru 'Ddu' a'r Ddalen 'Wen': Aralledd ac Amlddiwylliannedd mewn Ffuglen Gymreig, er 1990* ('Black' Wales and the 'White' Page; Otherness and Multiculturalism in Welsh Fiction, since 1990) (University of Wales Press, 2018).

Titles under discussion

Fiction

Azzopardi, Trezza, *The Hiding Place* (new ed., Picador, 2001[2000])

Bianchi, Tony, *Cyffesion Geordie Oddi Cartref* (Gwasg Gomer, 2010) (some stories from this collection are translated by the author and available in his story selection, *Staring Back at Me*, Cinnamon Press, 2018)

Lalwani, Nikita, *Gifted* ([2007]; Penguin, 2008)

Morgan, Mihangel, *Pan Oeddwn Fachgen* (Y Lolfa, 2002)

Price, Angharad, *Caersaint* (Y Lolfa, 2010).

Williams, Charlotte, *Sugar and Slate* (Planet, 2002)

Further reading

Aaron, Jane and Chris Williams, editors, *Postcolonial Wales* (University of Wales Press, 2005)

Anderson, Benedict, *Imagined Communities: Reflections of the Origin and Spread of Nationalism* (revised ed., Verso, 2006 [1983])

Baines, Menna, 'Y Saint yn eu gogoniant: holi Angharad Price am ei nofel newydd', *Barn*, 566 (March 2010), 33–4

Bhabha, Homi K., *The Location of Culture* (Routledge, 1994)

Bohata, Kirsti, *Postcolonialism Revisited* (University of Wales Press, 2004)

Brooks, Simon and Roberts, Richard Glyn, editors, *Pa Beth yr Aethoch Allan i'w Achub: Ysgrifau i Gynorthwyo'r Gwrthsafiad yn erbyn Dadfeiliad y Gymru Gymraeg* (Gwasg Carreg Gwalch, 2013)

Butler, Judith, *Bodies That Matter: On the Discursive Limits of 'Sex'* (Routledge, 1993)

Evans, Neil, Paul O'Leary, and Charlotte Williams, editors, *A Tolerant Nation?: Exploring Ethnic Diversity in Wales* (University of Wales Press, 2003)

Evans, Neil, Paul O'Leary, and Charlotte Williams, editors, *A Tolerant Nation?: Revisiting Ethnic Diversity in a Devolved Wales* (University of Wales Press, 2015)

Fanon, Frantz, *Black Skin, White Masks*, trans. Charles Lam Markmann ([1952]; new impression, Pluto, 2008 [1986])

Farris, Wendy B., *Ordinary Enchantments: Magical Realism and the Remystification of Narrative* (Vanderbilt University Press, 2004)

Higham, Gwennan, *Creu Dinasyddiaeth i Gymru: Mewnfudo Rhyngwladol a'r Gymraeg* (University of Wales Press, 2020)

James, Dafydd, 'Y Queer yn erbyn y Byd', *Taliesin*, 151 (Spring 2014), 66–85

Jones, Richard Wyn and Roger Scully, *Wales Says Yes: Devolution and the 2011 Welsh Referendum* (University of Wales Press, 2012)

Loomba, Ania, *Colonialism/Postcolonialism* (Routledge, 1998)

Macaulay, Thomas Babington, *Minute by the Hon'ble T.B. Macaulay, dated the 2nd February 1835*. Available: http://www.columbia.edu/itc/mealac/pritchett/00generallinks/macaulay/txt_minute_education_1835.html (accessed 4 January 2015)

Roberts, Gwyneth Tyson, *The Language of the Blue Books: Wales and Colonial Prejudice* (University of Wales Press, 2011)

Said, Edward W., *Reflections on Exile and Other Essays* (Harvard University Press, 2000)

Sheppard, Lisa, *Y Gymru 'Ddu' a'r Ddalen 'Wen': Aralledd ac Amlddiwyllianedd mewn Ffuglen Gymreig, er 1990* (University of Wales Press, 2018)

Thomas, M. Wynn, *Corresponding Cultures* (University of Wales Press, 1999)

Thomas, M. Wynn, editor, *DiFfinio Dwy Lenyddiaeth Cymru* (Gwasg Prifysgol Cymru, 1995)

Williams, Daniel G., *Wales Unchained: Literature, Politics and Identity in the American Century* (University of Wales Press, 2015)

Can Here be Home?
Putting Yourself Back
into 'the Other'

*Developing, with young people,
a series of diverse Welsh-language novellas*

Can Here be Home?
Putting Yourself Back
into 'the Other'

Elgan Rhys on developing, with young people,
a series of diverse Welsh-language novellas

Siwan Rosser's report (2017, see Siwan's article above) made several far-reaching recommendations to the Books Council's Grants Panel. Among those was the need for original material for young adults. As novel sequences were successful for this age group, and those were difficult to accomplish quickly in Welsh because of the need for authors to make their living elsewhere, the idea of developing a writing model similar to a television series was often debated. This would entail an editor developing characters, a storyline and synopsis for other authors to take up in individual novels which could be produced in series at a brisk pace. There was considerable excitement when Elgan contacted the Grants Department with a similar proposal rooted in the world of theatre and television. The panel agreed to award special project funding to the proposal and followed its development with enthusiasm. Of course, the topical and diverse situations and characters were also welcomed, but the method of working was particularly scrutinised to see if it could become a template for others. This is Elgan's account of how Y Pump (The Five) was realised, thereby providing an accessible platform for new, diverse voices; experience for budding Welsh-language authors, and a model for alternative publishing.

> Does home have to be a house of walls and windows? What about wherever I feel happy? Can here be home?
> Here. Where everything makes sense.
>
> *Aniq*, Marged Elen Wiliam with Mahum Umer

I am writing this at a strange time in our history and finding it difficult to shake off the bittersweet feeling. There is a chink of light as we slowly tread towards freedom from lockdowns, with a perception of future living experiences, but there is also hopelessness. With every step on our own, and together, we meet a variety of social, political and environmental challenges that have emerged over the last months. The future before us cries out for justice, harmony and solutions; solutions that can only be found if we succeed in applying that which is integral to us all: empathy.

For me, empathy will only be achieved if we set aside the space and time to *really* listen, watch and/or read others' living experiences, those stories which are different to ours, voices which are unfamiliar to our world. And despite the unfamiliarity and the very difference of these voices, it is possible, indeed likely, that we will surprise ourselves by discovering common and harmonious elements, even if those are, on the surface, comparatively unremarkable features.

But how do we get to experience those other stories, voices and living experiences?

That is the questions that I have asked myself constantly during these times. And there is a wider question: how do we reach those different stories that exist within our own Welsh culture? How do we reach those stories in the Welsh language? Do we have to wait for them to reach the shelves of our local bookshops?

One thing I have learnt during this period, as a white, middle-class, gay Welshman, is that there is no time to wait. And there is no time to be complacent about our privileges. Privileges; now that is a concept that has *really* come to the forefront of millions of people's minds during these last years. And in order to support the fight for justice, I have learnt that I *must* use my privileges to the best of my ability in order to give a voice to those who have been voiceless until now, and support them to share their stories.

My hope is that the series Y Pump, and its characters, will be part of this action.

> We are all one big orange laugh [...] And I want to pause time now, but I can't. So, I decide to remember this moment, forever, because *this* is what the Five is, isn't it? Us as one, and no one else in our world in this moment. Just us.
>
> *Tim,* Elgan Rhys with Tomos Jones

Y Pump is a series of novels about young peoples' experiences today, created collaboratively between five authors and five young co-authors, with myself as the creative director and editor of the series, Y Lolfa's priceless encouragement as publisher and Manon Steffan Ros's incredible mind as creative mentor. It seems that such a collaborative process is an exceptional one in our publishing industry (in the Welsh-language, at least), but I hope it offers a new way to enable young varied voices to lead in those stories that are published.

As someone who is new to the book industry, my hope is to bring a fresh perspective from my experience in a very different sector. With the skills I have gained in leading and experimenting with cooperative projects, I hope to contribute towards creating a more inclusive sector. One of the project's other aims is to foster leadership skills and to encourage young people's own ambitions to lead future collaborative projects, to see their efforts bear fruit, each leaf burning with passion.

To give a little of my background before Y Pump. After completing a graduate course in Theatre and Drama in the University of South Wales in 2013, I set about trying to create my own opportunities. I was keen to create new theatre pieces, as I found it difficult to find the opportunities and space to develop the kind of work I was interested in creating. That is to say: theatre which experimented with multilingualism (Welsh, English and any other language), theatre which examined devised processes and theatre which was inspired by the stories of the various individuals, communities and cultures of Wales. Over time, I discovered that if you were sure what you needed and wanted to create something, but were unsure of *how* to achieve that, you had to find the people or companies that could offer help and support. And that is what I did: asking the Sherman Theatre, where I was working in the ticket office, for support to research an idea for a show. The rest is history as they say.

Since then, I have jointly established and led Cwmni Pluen Company, a theatre company that creates multilingual, devised performances by examining the various stories of this country we live in. We created the company's first show *Llais/Voice* (2014), before proceeding to devise three other shows, *Ti.Me* (2015), *Mags* (2018) and *UsProclaimed/ClywchNi* (2017) with Mess Up the Mess, and then a show in development with the National Eisteddfod, *Corn Gwlad* (2019).

As well as my work with Pluen, over recent years I have worked with theatre companies such as Frân Wen, Theatr Iolo, National Theatre Wales, Theatr Genedlaethol Cymru, Sherman Theatre and Theatr Clwyd – and each time the process has been a little different. However, I have been lucky enough to have had transformational personal experiences in my professional career, for example, on a project about the evolution of my friendship with a childhood friend, and another involving working with a group of older women, with whom I am still in contact. Each one has had some long-term effect on me as I came to better understand myself and my relationship with the world. One example is when I came out as a result of the show *Llais/Voice*, an important turning point in dealing with my sexuality.

In doing so, I set down a strong, collaborative, emotional foundation for my work. I decided that as I progressed with my career, this would be at the heart of every piece I would create: and central to that is giving a fitting platform to the stories of those who consider their voices to be less valued.

> We just kind of ended up in the same group none of us quite fits the norm, whatever slant you take on that. Of course, I love each one of them to bloody bits and we depend on each other so much, but I just ask myself sometimes whether it's a natural thing, us being drawn to each other, or whether it's society forcing that on us. Whichever it is, I'm glad.
>
> *Tami,* Mared Roberts with Ceri-Anne Gatehouse

Y Pump is a series of five novels for young people, about five characters in Year 11 who have come together because they feel that they have been alienated; Tim because of his autism, Tami because of her movement disability, Aniq her faith, Robin his sexuality and last of all, Cat, with her illness. Each novel follows the timetable of the school year, with five authors in their twenties telling the experience of a different character in each novel. Above all else, it is all created in collaboration with five young co-authors. But why 'above all else'? Why collaborate with co-authors? And what is the benefit of such collaboration?

At the start of the process of putting Y Pump together, we were keen to secure five confident, experienced and varied authors who could offer differing perspectives, who could indentify directly with the living experiences of the series' characters, and, especially, who could identify with the attributes that play a part in the characters' feelings of alienation.

This proved to be troublesome. Immersing myself into the usual networks of the publishing world and meeting several authors on Zoom, it became clear that there *was* a variety of authors with wide perspectives, but scarcely any that I contacted could identify with the characters' attributes. This was a moment of revelation to me. One which meant that the project had to look for a wider strategy than that of the project itself. A strategy that could uncover Welsh voices who *did* identify with the characters, and give them a platform and opportunity so that they could share their stories and follow a path as a Welsh-language author. The authors are there, but we need to go beyond the sector, beyond our habits, in order to uncover and invite in the new, contemporary and authentic voices in today's Wales.

So, I decided that I would myself write one novel and that I would recruit four of the authors I had contacted over Zoom, namely Mared Roberts, Marged Elen Wiliam, Iestyn Tyne and Megan Angharad Hunter, all sensitive, empathetic and collaborative authors. While the five of us offer wide perspectives, there is a common element uniting us: our privileges, as white, university-educated Welsh speakers. Therefore, we undertook to collaborate closely with young authors along the way and to be completely open to being challenged and educated ourselves in terms of what affects people who are different to us in many ways.

> I'm trying to stay in the feeble shadow of the tree, but I'm enjoying this view too much to leave. Tim on his back in the grass looking for shapes in the clouds. Tami sipping from her water bottle as if it was an expensive cocktail with a pink umbrella stuck in it. Robyn trying to make a daisy chain from the little flowers wilting in the heat. And Cat like a model in her sunglasses, soaking up the sun's rays, her head resting on Robyn's lap.
>
> *Aniq*, Marged Elen Wiliam with Mahum Umer

The next step was to find the co-authors. This stage was both exciting and frightening. I could not wait to reach new voices, but was also concerned that the message would not reach beyond my usual networks and the book trade. I already knew I would have to look beyond those sectors and only one place felt right for the first step – social media. With the generous help of the Urdd to spread the message, after one tweet and one Instagram story, almost forty young people expressed an interest in the project, and almost every one of those indentified with the living experiences of one or more of the characters in some way. I was knocked out by all the messages. I remember thinking, once again, the authors *are* there, after all. Looking for their chance to share their stories.

Unfortunately, there was only room for five co-authors on the project. Picking and choosing was very difficult, but after reading samples of the varied work of the young people, I was very proud, and still feel privileged, to collaborate with Tomos, Ceri-Anne, Mahum, Leo and Maisie – without these five, then Y Pump would not be The Five. Every other young person was invited to join a database for other art organisations and to participate in the first Zoom workshop with all the authors, Manon Steffan Ros and myself, and to contribute to the initial decisions about our fictional world: the world of Y Pump.

Following this first workshop, there was a busy, thorough and ambitious timetable for the authors and co-authors. A period of writing for the authors, followed by Zoom workshops with the co-authors responding to the work. The co-authors were also part of mentoring sessions on the publishing trade with Y Lolfa and marketing sessions with AM (amam.cymru, a digital, cultural multi-channel community), as well as workshops with myself and Manon to develop their own writing, which is now published on AM. It was important for me that the co-authors also had the opportunity to develop and publish their own original writing during the process, and could own a piece of work to be proud of.

As well as this work, the co-authors were part of email conversations discussing their characters' attributes, and to share their views on the drafts of Steffan Dafydd's glorious covers. We were very aware that the time the project was taking up in these individuals' lives, therefore the principle that the co-authors should be paid was something that I and Y Lolfa were determined to act upon.

I was very proud when the Arts Council of Wales approved the project, and invested its confidence in myself and Y Lolfa to take a lead, but even more so when they were prepared to invest in new voices.

> Me in my shawl and her in her scarf, all colours, and sitting there, and a lot, a lot, of questions between us but they can wait until after, or another day or time. I just want to look at the sea for a while, like I'm always doing. And think about New York.
>
> And I look at her, Aniq, as well, quietly without her realising, because she's mesmerised by the sea. And I think about how much she's had to say goodbye to. And I squeeze her hand, and she squeezes mine right back, as if she was thinking exactly the same thing.
>
> *Robyn,* Iestyn Tyne with Leo Drayton

This set a precedent and helped make the project equitable, a characteristic of all elements of this project, including the idea of having the names of the authors and co-authors the same size on the novels' covers – the little things are important.

And the little things *are* important on the project, because there is hope beyond Y Pump itself. As we travel towards a future which cries out for justice, my hope is that this project will encourage other such collaborations in the future and that the book sector will come up with imaginative and innovative ways of working together to make sure that the shelves of our bookshops *really* reflect our Wales, today.

While I have not referenced the authors of the series to any great degree in this article, naturally this is not because their time or voices are less valuable. I would like to thank Mared, Marged, Iestyn and Megan enormously for their sensitivity, their generosity and their willingness to collaborate, listen and give their time to the co-authors in order to enrich, influence and guide their work. Thanks also for the mastery of their craft.

I want to read novels by our co-authors: Tomos Jones, Ceri-Anne Gatehouse, Mahum Umer, Leo Drayton, Maisie Awen and all the young people I had the privilege of meeting over Zoom or on the phone during barren times. Our literary future will not be barren if it is in their hands.

And then we all laugh and you know you're best friends with
someone when you can laugh with each other out of *nowhere*,
even without even saying anything, and *this*.
This is the best feeling in the world.

Cat, Megan Angharad Hunter with Maisie Awen

For me, Y Pump is full of voices, moments of closeness and authentic stores
which are rich and reflect the experiences of young people in Wales today.
When the world feels like it is forcing us to be separate – literally, politically,
geographically, environmentally – I really hope that Tim, Tami, Aniq, Robyn and
Cat offer young people the opportunity to remember the power of friendship
and demand a platform and space for their own honest expression.

This project has been one of the highlights of my career up to now, without
a doubt. I hope that Y Pump will germinate more voices and experimental ways
of creating collaborative, exciting work for the young people of Wales.

Thank you so much for today; if the rest of the project is half as good
as today was, it will be one of the highlights of my life so far.

Tomos, email after our first Zoom workshop

Elgan Rhys is a writer, director and performer. He is the editor and
creative director of the brand new series, Y Pump, namely *Aniq* by
Marged Elen Wiliam with Mahum Umer, *Tim* by Elgan Rhys with Tomos
Jones, *Tami* by Mared Roberts with Ceri-Anne Gatehouse, *Robyn* by
Iestyn Tyne with Leo Drayton and *Cat* by Megan Angharad Hunter with
Maisie Awen. These short novels, by young people for young people,
are available from Y Lolfa as separate titles or as a box set.

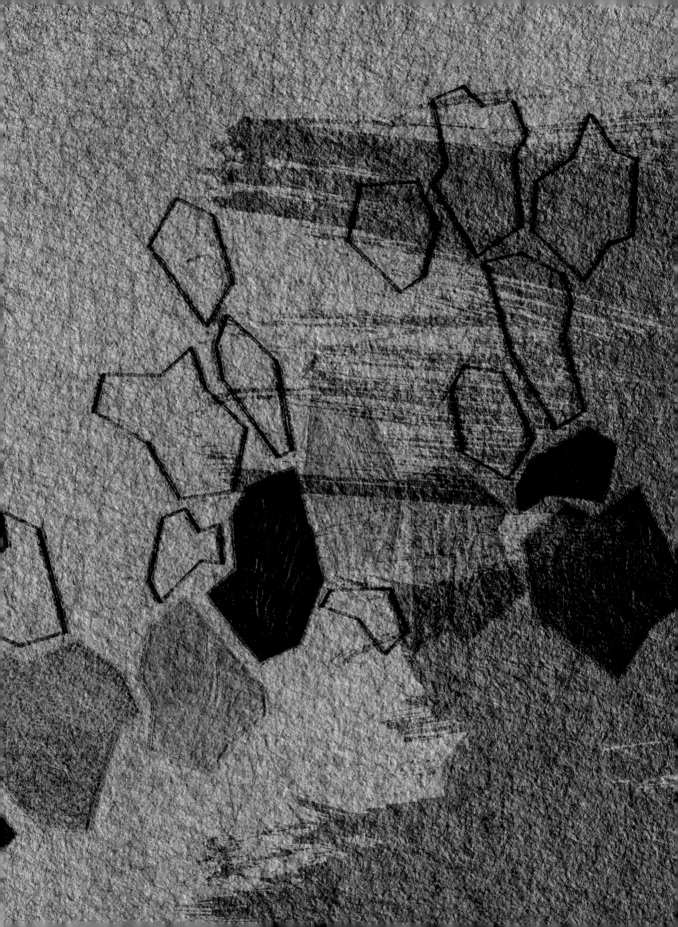

Hearsay, Mis-history and the Bear's Head

Editing the diverse essay collections
Just So You Know *and* Welsh (plural)

Hearsay, Mis-history and the Bear's Head

Hanan Issa on editing the diverse essay collections
Just So You Know *and* Welsh (plural)

I grew up in Penarth, a seaside commuter town next to Cardiff. A red-and-gold sign above the town's main pub reads 'The Bear's Head'. This is a designation inspired by the long-held belief that the town's name is a mangled version of two Welsh words: 'pen' meaning 'head' and 'arth' meaning 'bear'. The Penarthian bear's origin is a subject often debated. It's been suggested that the shape of Penarth on a map resembled the head of a bear before the inevitable sea erosion to its cliffs. Others claim that there was an actual bear living in the woodlands that once covered the area. The telling and retelling of these half-truths has even infiltrated the town's crest that to this day features two upright bears.[1] If you walk up the hill from the Victorianesque pier and promenade, past the enviably situated sea-facing houses, there's a path to the headland that juts out to sea. On clear days, you can see across the channel to the twin islands, Flat Holm and Steep Holm. This headland, or promontory to be totally accurate, is the 'pennardd' my town is named for.[2] Not a bear in sight. Perhaps the 'Mandela effect' permeation of my hometown's history is why I'm drawn to creating work where fiction, place, language, and history intersects.

My debut poetry pamphlet, *My Body Can House Two Hearts*, was very much, as Octavio Paz puts it, a 'constellation of blood'.[3] The poems, mostly concerned with making sense of my identity as a mixed-race Welsh Arab, had taken up space in my mind for a long time. Some were in different forms before finding themselves on the pages of my pamphlet. Some arrived almost fully formed. As a writer, I've never been very good at writing every day. I much prefer to sit with an idea first. I'll read, cook, exercise, give my son a bath – anything but write. The idea, whether it's a poem or a story, prefers to sit in the background, percolating. I don't know if I've settled on this process because it is the optimal way of writing for my particular brain. Or if it's just because, as a young mother, I don't tend to have the luxury of sitting at my desk all day, purely to write. But when I am sat at my desk, I've become accustomed to expecting constant interruption. There's a gesture I've unconsciously picked up from my dad: the shaking of a partially closed fist, thumb touching your index finger, which means 'give me five minutes'. My son, as you can imagine, hates this gesture, I'm guessing because he is the one subjected to it most. But my hand remembers the movement a lot quicker than the mind-cluttering process of saying the words out loud. Though I'm not sure if this half-remembered gesture is actually a part of nonverbal Arabic vocabulary, or if it is just that our family has absorbed it into our own shared language.

Early in 2020, just before the pandemic, I was sitting in Tŷ Newydd, north Wales with a collection of English and Welsh-speaking creatives from Where I'm Coming From (WICF, an open-mic series) and *Y Stamp* magazine. Kindly invited to attend by Literature Wales, we spent the morning translating each other's poetry from Welsh to English and English to Welsh. We then moved onto discussing how the word 'intersectionality' tastes on a Welsh tongue. The native Welsh speakers are poets, so the conversation danced between practicalities and beauty. Cydgyfeirioldeb – a convergence; rhyngblethu – interweaving. We stop and acknowledge the moment: of ancient language remade, of history unfolding. A year later and we are at the close of the Hunan-Iaith project, an Arts Council-funded venture by *Y Stamp* and WICF to build an accessible vocabulary for Welsh speakers to discuss issues of race and identity. Raymond Williams, in his powerful work, *Keywords: A Vocabulary of Culture and Society* says:

Our possibilities for criticism and productivity are absolutely inseparable from the existence of a common vocabulary.

The more I think about this, the more convinced I am that he would celebrate the aims of the Hunan-Iaith project, namely to enhance our cultural discussions of race and identity, Wales and belonging, by providing Welsh-language speakers with the lexical tools necessary to have these discussions.

In Parthian's anthology, *Just So You Know: Essays of Experience*,[4] each of the contributors gift us with a kind of vocabulary, a glimpse into their life at the point of converging identities: Welshness, disability, mental health, race, religion etc. To be Welsh and Queer, Welsh and Black: titles that multiply with prefixes and suffixes, spaces with unfamiliar faces. I think if this anthology had been compiled a decade ago, the purpose would have been to inform the default white, heterosexual identity of life on the other side. But *Just So You Know* doesn't seek to educate; as the title implies, it is an archiving of experience. Those voices within extend a hand to the 'othered'. Unapologetically taking up space on a page, in a book, on a Welsh bookstore's shelf, as proof that Welshness can flourish, devoid of slate, coal or sheep. While editing, I was struck by how effortlessly these essays construct a Welshness that is both familiar and not. Ruqaya Izzidien's essay in the anthology, titled 'The Other Side' captures the struggle of being mixed race and having multiple loyalties. Two roads that have diverged in a wood are personified in her account of leading her entire Welsh comprehensive school in a protest against the war in Iraq. Kandace Siobhan Walker deftly weaves together strands of Welsh and Kenyan mythology in her essay, 'Everything I Will Give You'. This tapestry, alive with the shifting figures of women and water, ripples across a legendary landscape. Shaken out, shaking up, it is made and made anew.

Much like the myth of Penarth's bear's head, the Welsh literary scene was once told and re-told as a place lacking in diverse talent. Institutions would shake their heads at the hopeless search for underrepresented stories. But Durre Shahwar

– my WICF co-founder – and I knew this wasn't true. We were here, in Wales, writing and performing our own work. There had to be others. And there were. Where I'm Coming From has seen a steady influx of creative individuals who were previously deemed non-existent, right from its inception. We are a constantly growing collective that is also shaped like a headland, our voices resounding across the sea. But this doesn't mean we haven't had to fight the beast. The problems we have encountered include hulking disdain for our collective's platforming of new and untried writers, teeth bared when we refuse to allow microaggressions to go unchallenged. Snarling threats to end our career in this roiling pond – where everyone knows the names of each other's children – have come and gone.

But I get weary of wearing the armour required to fight a daily fight. Sometimes I want to write about birdsong or what my son eats for tea. When reality is such a struggle, there's comfort in the escapist merging of myth and the mundane. I have an Iraqi heritage but my family dynamic means I don't have much opportunity to learn about that side of myself. So instead, I google, read, and fantasise as much as I can. I half-remember a bedtime story about a monstrous river witch called the Si'luwa. Often mistaken for a hairy ape or bear, she lives on an invisible floating island lost in a maze on the Hammar marshes in Southern Iraq. I write a poem for her, a sympathetic love letter, since I see myself in her misunderstood-ness. I take my son to the Artes Mundi exhibition at the National Museum in Cardiff, where we encounter the artist Firelei Baez's mysterious Ciguapa: a figure with overgrown glossy hair and feathers painted over maps of the colonial world. Remaking history, the Ciguapa/Si'luwa figure that manifests itself in many other cultures' folklore, convinces me that everywhere in the world, people like to make monsters of strong women. I see myself being made and remade by the experiences I have – the good and bad – all those experiences sticking to my legs in feathery clumps, sprouting like vines from my back. Such hybridisation, however, is not always something to be celebrated.

The Mabinogi's Blodeuwedd was punished with the feathery form of an owl. That feeling, of being squeezed by others into a particular shape, comes upon me often when hearing or taking part in discussion about identity. Must I become the bear's head, because that is what people think they see and what half-baked knowledge, mis-learnt history and repeated rumour dictate? A few years ago, I was asked to share an experience of Islamophobia with a news outlet. I saw it as a positive story, since I had had an unusually supportive response from the police and wanted to encourage others facing abuse to speak up and seek help. But, unfortunately, that was not the narrative the newsroom wanted. Instead, the segment was filled with mournful music and side shots of my face, unsmiling, filmed between takes. I promised myself I would not allow others to reframe my story like that again. As a freelance writer, this has been tricky, since there are often commission requests that want you to excavate that trauma for the white gaze. It's no coincidence that books like *Not Without My Daughter*[5] are still displayed prominently on supermarket bestseller shelves. Admittedly, it can sometimes boil down to how much is in my bank account, but tattooed at the back of my mind is Toni Morrison's warning:

> The function, the very serious function of racism is distraction.
> It keeps you from doing your work. It keeps you explaining, over
> and over again, your reason for being.

Having many times fallen into that trap of explaining, I'd like to think I've learnt something of how to prevent repeating that mistake. Initially, I thought this meant avoiding any work that focused on my racial or religious identity, but this felt odd and I again sensed that I was being stuffed into a particular shape, albeit this time by my own self-limitation. Instead, I've relaxed into a state perfectly summarised by the artist Carrie Mae Weems. In a Covid-induced Zoom event organised by Artes Mundi, Weems talked about 'creating art that you absolutely need to see'.

Last year, I was discussing the problem of Blodeuwedd's story arc with Welsh animator, Efa Blosse-Mason. Although she is now recognised as one of the most popular characters of the Mabinogi, Blodeuwedd's simple purpose seems to be as companion for the main character of the story, Lleu Llaw Gyffes. When she rejects this fate, she is punished. Her beauty, constructed by man for man, is reversed. Efa and I envisioned the character's life in modern society. Rejecting second-hand decrepit distortions of old woman and owl, we needed to see her as triumphant against the Trumps of this world. And so, in our animated poetry film, *Blodeuwedd's Gift*,[6] part of the BBC New Creatives scheme, we have reimagined Blodeuwedd as a monstrous fairy godmother, who keeps a protective watch over the city as her daughters walk home alone at night.

Firelei Baez, one of the current Artes Mundi artists, speaks about being in a constant state of 'becoming'.[7] This resonates within my most creative depths. The word 'creative' comes from the Latin 'crescere', meaning 'to grow'. I grow and become. I become and grow. The stories of my past meld myth and history until I am no longer sure which is which. The face of an Islamophobia victim or the dreaded Ciguapa? A head of the land or head of a bear? Though, to be honest, I'm not as interested in those binaries as I am in the possibility of reimagining how these faces, heads, necks and bodies can be stitched together.

At the time of writing, I am co-editing an essay anthology entitled *Welsh (plural)* to be published in spring 2022 by Repeater Books, with Darren Chetty, Grug Muse, and Iestyn Tyne as co-editors. Contributors, including Joe Dunthorne, Charlotte Williams, and Niall Griffiths, were asked to envisage a future Wales that is both distinct and inclusive. Reimagined and radical, *Welsh (plural)* is an appropriate successor to Parthian's *Just So You Know*, transforming Welsh voices from archive-echoes to attempted prophecy. And looking to the future feels very necessary in a world slowly crawling out of the clutches of Covid. My own essay contribution centres on whether the identities of being Welsh and being Muslim intersect. Charlotte Williams, in conversation with Darren Chetty, talks about a civic sense of identity: 'I'm putting in. I'm here. I'm part of this story today and I'm making a claim on it.'[8] In my essay, I express the hope that this 'putting in' becomes more of a prevalent marker of Welsh identity in the future, and in so doing, rewrites past maps of belonging. Such a civic identity, so clearly advocated by Williams, may, for some, evoke – at a national level – the founding ideas of contemporary Welsh and Scottish nationalism. The extent to which civic identity in Wales is a power for inclusivity has been slow to gain traction.

Perhaps that is because of the myth, mis-history and hearsay that gave the Bear's Head its name? In any case, ideas about identity and belonging that are above all fluid, open up a place for a Penarthian-Iraqi writer like me, who is constantly searching for ways to explore, remake, and reimagine.

Hanan Issa is a writer, poet and artist from Wales. Her debut pamphlet, *My Body Can House Two Hearts*, was published by Burning Eye Books. Her work has been performed and published on platforms such as BBC Wales, ITV Wales, Huffington Post, StAnza festival, *Poetry Wales*, Wales Arts International and the British Council. Her winning monologue was performed at the Bush Theatre as part of the Hijabi Monologues. She was co-editor of *Just So You Know: Essays of Experience* (published by Parthian, a core-funded revenue client of the Books Council of Wales) and is the co-founder of Where I'm Coming From open-mic series. She has collaborated on short film commissions with BBC New Creatives and National Dance Company Wales and is a recipient of the 2020 Ffolio, Ffilm Cymru/BBC Wales short film commission. She is currently part of Literature Wales' Representing Wales Writer Development Scheme as well as co-editing *Welsh (plural)*, an essay anthology including Darren Chetty, Grug Muse, and Iestyn Tyne, forthcoming from Repeater Books.

Notes

[1] http://thevaleofglamorgan.com/history/index.htm.

[2] Hywel Wyn Jones, *The Place-Names of Wales* (University of Wales Press: 2015).

[3] Octavio Paz, *Toward the Poem*, in Robin D.G. Kelley, *Freedom Dreams: The Black Radical Imagination* (Beacon Press: 2003).

[4] *Just So You Know: Essays of Experience,* edited by Hanan Issa, Durre Shahwar, and Özgür Uyanik (Parthian, 2020).

[5] Betty Mahmoody, *Not Without My Daughter* (Corgi [New Ed.], July 2004).

[6] Blodeuwedd's Gift, https://vimeo.com/455217900.

[7] Papyarose, Artist Interview with Firelei Baez, https://www.papayarose.com/home/2019/2/24/artist-interview-firelei-baez.

[8] Darren Chetty, 'Charlotte Williams in Conversation', *Wales Arts Review* (2021): https://www.walesartsreview.org/charlotte-williams-in-conversation/.

Titles for Six Decades

At the start of each chapter you will find the cover of a book title, either Welsh language or of Welsh interest, each published between 1961 and 2021, as follows. Thanks to the publishers, artists and designers for their permissions, where that is relevant, and thanks to The National Library of Wales for their help in supplying some of the covers. Titles selected by Gwen Davies.

Page 218: A Child's Christmas in Wales Dylan Thomas (Dent, 1968), woodcuts
by Ellen Raskin

Page 228: Laboratories of the Spirit RS Thomas (Gwasg Gregynog, 1976), fine binding
by Sally Lou Smith, with permission of Gwasg Gregynog and University if Wales
Trinity Saint David, supplied by The National Library of Wales

Translations, including literary translation of quotations
Chapters 2 to 10, in addition to chapters 12 and 13, Rhidian Griffiths
and Gwen Davies Literary Services
Chapter 1, 11, 14, 15 and 16, Gwen Davies Literary Services

Linocuts by Molly Brown

Cover: 'Hazel'

Chapter 1: 'Autumn Garden'

Chapter 2: 'Buzzard and Gorse'

Chapter 3: 'Sunken Pathway'

Chapter 4: 'Carningli II'

Chapter 5: 'Cashew Apples'

Chapter 6: 'Two Rivers'

Chapter 7: 'Top of the Hill (bicycle)'

Chapter 8: 'Samphire and Seabeet'

Chapter 9: 'Coracle'

Chapter 10: 'Nevern Celtic Cross'

Chapter 11: 'Mangrove Apples'

Chapter 12: 'Fritillaries'

Chapter 13: 'Hazel'

Chapter 14: 'Banana Orchard'

Chapter 15: 'Bodaboda (motorbike)'

Chapter 16: 'Welsh Black Sheep'

Endpapers and title page: 'Hart's Tongue Fern' and 'Taro'

Thanks

The warmest thanks are due to the following people and institutions: M. Wynn Thomas, who had the original idea for a book that would celebrate the Books Council among other important Welsh institutions; the Creunant family, for their generous support towards this volume, and for the faithful and inspiring service given by Alun to the Council in the first place; the contributors; the publishers and bookshops of Wales; Molly Brown for her beautiful images; Olwen Fowler for her handsome design; Rhidian Griffiths for translating the original chapters in their original form; the artists and designers who contributed the original covers of the 'titles for six decades' featured here and to Sîon Ilar for designing many of them; Huw Meirion Edwards for editing the book's original draft; The National Library of Wales for supplying book covers, and to the Ceredigion Library Aberystwyth for research assistance.